The Grace of Playing

HORIZONS *IN* RELIGIOUS EDUCATION is a book series sponsored by the Religious Education Association: An Association of Professors, Practitioners and Researchers in Religious Education. It was established to promote new scholarship and exploration in the academic field of Religious Education. The series will include both seasoned educators and newer scholars and practitioners just establishing their academic writing careers.

Books in this series reflect religious and cultural diversity, educational practice, living faith, and the common good of all people. They are chosen on the basis of their contributions to the vitality of religious education around the globe. Writers in this series hold deep commitments to their own faith traditions, yet their work sets forth claims that might also serve other religious communities, strengthen academic insight, and connect the pedagogies of religious education to the best scholarship of numerous cognate fields.

The posture of the Religious Education Association has always been ecumenical and multi-religious, attuned to global contexts, and committed to affecting public life. These values are grounded in the very institutions, congregations, and communities that transmit religious faith. The association draws upon the interdisciplinary richness of religious education connecting theological, spiritual, religious, social science and cultural research and wisdom. Horizons of Religious Education aims to heighten understanding and appreciation of the depth of scholarship resident within the discipline of religious education, as well as the ways it impacts our common life in a fragile world. Without a doubt, we are inspired by the wonder of teaching and the awe that must be taught.

Jack L. Seymour (co-chair), Garrett-Evangelical Theological Seminary

Dean G. Blevins (co-chair), Nazarene Theological Seminary

Elizabeth Caldwell (co-chair), McCormick Theological Seminary

Dori Grinenko Baker, The Fund for Theological Education & Sweet Briar College

Sondra H. Matthaei, Saint Paul School of Theology

Siebren Miedema, Vrije Universiteit Amsterdam

Hosffman Ospino, Boston College

Mai-Anh Le Tran, Eden Theological Seminary

Anne Streaty Wimberly, Interdenominational Theological Seminary

The Grace of Playing

Pedagogies for Leaning into God's New Creation

COURTNEY T. GOTO

PICKWICK *Publications* · Eugene, Oregon

THE GRACE OF PLAYING
Pedagogies for Leaning into God's New Creation

Horizons in Religious Education

Pickwick Publications
An Imprint of Wipf and Stock Publishers
199 W. 8th Ave., Suite 3
Eugene, OR 97401

www.wipfandstock.com

ISBN 13: 978-1-4982-3300-2

Cataloging-in-Publication data:

Goto, Courtney T.

The grace of playing : pedagogies for leaning into God's new creation / Courtney T. Goto.

xxii + 150 p. ; 23 cm. —Includes bibliographical references.

Horizons in Religious Education

ISBN 13: 978-1-4982-3300-2

1. Teaching—Religious aspects—Christianity. 2. Play—Religious aspects—Christianity 3. Christian education—Philosophy. I. Title. II. Series.

BV1464 G77 2016

Manufactured in the U.S.A.

For Horton

CONTENTS

SERIES FOREWORD

Religious Education Association

HORIZONS in RELIGIOUS EDUCATION defines a book series sponsored by the Religious Education Association: An Association of Professors, Practitioners and Researchers in Religious Education. The REA founded this series to promote new scholarship and exploration in the academic field of Religious Education. The series includes both seasoned educators alongside newer scholars and practitioners just establishing their academic writing careers.

Books in this series reflect religious and cultural diversity, educational practice, living faith, and the common good of all people. They are chosen on the basis of their contributions to the vitality of religious education around the globe. Writers in this series hold deep commitments to their own faith traditions, yet their work sets forth claims that might also serve other religious communities, strengthen academic insight, and connect the pedagogies of religious education to the best scholarship of numerous cognate fields.

The posture of the Religious Education Association has always been ecumenical and multi-religious, attuned to global contexts, and committed to affecting public life. The REA establishes these values in the very institutions, congregations, and communities that transmit religious faith. The association draws upon the interdisciplinary richness of religious education connecting theological, spiritual, religious, social science, and cultural research and wisdom. *HORIZONS in RELIGIOUS EDUCATION* aims to heighten understanding and appreciation of the depth of scholarship resident within the discipline of religious education, as well as the ways it impacts our common life in a fragile world. Without a doubt, we are inspired by the wonder of teaching and the awe that must be taught.

—Dean Blevins, Former president of REA and Professor of Practical Theology and Christian Discipleship at Nazarene Theological Seminary in Kansas City, Missouri, U.S.A. Co-chair, Horizons Editorial Board

EDITORS' PREFACE

We are pleased to announce this third book in the REA HORIZONS series. Rooted in her own Christian tradition, Dr. Courtney Goto of Boston University School of Theology offers possibilities on which many religious educators from many religious traditions can draw. As we all have experienced, there are magnificent moments in good teaching/learning when insight and possibility "appear." In fact, as we teachers watch learners' faces and see ways they relate to one another, we see moments of revelation or confirmation as things come together and as new practices are tested in community—"ah-ha" moments. Out of confusion or ignorance comes clarity and possibilities. Using Christian theological language, Dr. Goto calls these moments "grace."

We all have seen these moments. We have experienced them ourselves. They are often a surprise. We had searched and searched for an answer, a meaning, or a connection with others. All of our searching however felt futile as little of value came. And, then, all of a sudden, connections are made and we "see!" New meanings, insights, and ways of being together emerge. Immediately a sense of joy washes over us and we know. As the Hebrew word, *yada*, "to know" makes very clear, knowing is a form of intimacy where two souls connect and share meanings at the deepest levels.

Through her practical theology of Christian religious education, Dr. Goto points us to the theological, historical, educational, and aesthetic sources that illustrate this intimate kind of learning. In profound ways, she connects devotional practices, spirituality, and visual art to show us that God is alive making things new, offering possibilities, and enfleshing our journeys with hope.

Learning experiences where connections are made can occur in the mundane and ordinary or in profound transformative moments. But no matter what, they point to the reality that humans are meaning-making creatures seeking community and working to shape a future that itself makes connections among humans and all creation. We are constantly "leaning into" God's new creation.

Dr. Goto's work stands in a long line of theologians and religious educators who have taught us the power of spirit, of play, and of the creative imagination to offer hope and life. Theologies of hope and culture ground her work. Educators who saw the possibilities of the imagination in thought, word, and deed inform it. And her faith points us to the meaning of God as the one that works for, imagines, and offers new creation, even when we are most frustrated and fear there are no options or hope. Gracious learning emboldens us to seek new life and to extend it.

We commend this book to you. It connects with previous books in the REA HORIZONS series, Sheryl Kujawa-Holbrook's *God beyond Borders* and Sarah Tauber's *Open Minds, Devoted Hearts*, as it seeks to offer us concrete ways to affect our public world. Religious education at its best is grounded in a particular religious tradition, it connects that tradition with the realities of living, and it offers ways that we can work together to reshape, redeem, and transform the world into a more whole and Holy place.

As Dr. Goto describes, good education is "standing on Holy ground"—people are opened to new insights, connections among strangers are built, directions to work for community and hope are revealed, and we are encouraged to continue the struggle for new life, even in the midst of loss, brokenness, and failure. Join in the play: find new words and concepts to understand the grace of insight and join in the art of shaping our world and our futures together.

—Jack L. Seymour, Professor Emeritus of Religious Education at Garrett-Evangelical Theological Seminary, Evanston, Illinois, U.S.A. Co-chair, Horizons Editorial Board

—Elizabeth Caldwell, Harold Blake Walker Professor Emerita of Pastoral Theology of McCormick Theological Seminary in Chicago, Illinois, U.S.A. Co-chair, Horizons Editorial Board

HORIZONS IN RELIGIOUS EDUCATION— EDITORIAL REVIEW BOARD

AUTHOR'S PREFACE

WHEN GOD'S NEW CREATION SHINES THROUGH

When teaching enlivens learners and they feel, see, or know something new, learning is an experience of grace, a receipt of an unexpected gift. A veil is lifted; scales fall from the eyes. These are rare, precious moments in teaching and learning, moments that cannot be predicted or orchestrated. They usually occur when participants in a learning community engage one another deeply and authentically. Then the space of teaching is holy ground; then learners encounter Spirit and the teacher is not fully in control.[1] When this happens, it is as if a bit of God's new creation shines through. Learners and teachers alike experience a glimpse of the new people that they can be and become, the new reality in which they are being called to participate. Such moments inspire religious educators to invite revelatory experiencing.

For centuries, religious educators have drawn on creative inspiration and practical wisdom to facilitate such revelatory experiencing that deeply moves learners. Missionaries taught through fairs and exhibits, wordless books, and lantern slides. In the late 1930s at Howard University, Howard Thurman staged life-sized tableaux of great works of art, complete with "living Madonnas."[2] In the mid-1940s, he incorporated liturgical dance into worship at the Church of the Fellowship of All Peoples in San Francisco, then at Boston University's Marsh Chapel in the 1950s.[3] As a professor at Drew University from 1956 to 1971, Nelle Morton used "story,

---

1. For more on embodying grace in teaching, see Boys, "Grace of Teaching."
2. Thurman, *With Head and Heart*, 94–95.
3. Ibid., 148; photo and caption between 46–47.

drama, dance, art, and role-play" in her teaching.[4] In the 1960s, 70s, and 80s, churches witnessed ordinary Christians teaching adults through performance art such as clown ministry, liturgical dance, and biblical drama. In more recent decades, religious educators have used digital technology in the service of making disciples.

All such efforts reflect a yearning for a more "holistic, lived-experience model of education,"[5] one that builds on the ideas of George Albert Coe, Sophia Lyon Fahs, William Clayton Bower, and others.[6] Already in 1929 Coe argued, "[W]e cannot maintain vital continuity with Jesus unless we do take his road of discovery and creation."[7] Convinced that the faithful need to be creators with Jesus, he wrote of church people "evoking the unprecedented by our own thinking, experimenting, daring and suffering. Reconstruction, continuous reconstruction, is of the essence of the divine work in and through the human."[8] Coe recognized the importance of having others' help in awakening humans to faith, which I believe is at the heart of revelatory experiencing. He wrote, "[T]here can be no purely private relation to God, for our very selfhood is conjunct. We are made selves by a give-and-take with others and we are made in [God's] image."[9]

It has not been easy developing and practicing alternatives to a "schooling model of education," which has influenced the educational culture, imagination, and assumptions of teachers of every kind, including some religious educators.[10] Likewise, many theorists in religious education have taken up Paulo Freire's critique of the "banking" style of teaching in search of more integrated, experiential, and creative learning.[11] Rather than adopting a schooling model in which learning is separated from the rest of life,[12] some religious educators have called for an understanding of the "congregation as educator," in which the entire life of the congregation and its practices serve as opportunities for Christian formation.[13] In other

4. Caldwell, "Nelle Morton," 54.

5. Brelsford, "Schooling Model," 357.

6. See Moore, *Continuity and Change*, 29–30; also Boys, *Educating in Faith*, 52–55.

7. Coe, *What is Christian Education?* 33.

8. Ibid.; Boys, *Educating in Faith*, 52.

9. Coe, *What is Christian Education?* 73.

10. Brelsford, "Schooling Model," 357.

11. Freire, *Pedagogy of the Oppressed*.

12. Brelsford, "Schooling Model," 357.

13. Hinds, "Congregation as Educator," 79–93; Proffitt, Gilmour, and Prevost, "The Congregation as Educator," 294–415; Lee, *Transforming Congregations*.

instances, instead of relying heavily on a linguistic transfer of knowledge, some scholars have turned their attention to aesthetic teaching[14] or reclaimed notions of conversion[15] or practices of contemplation and liturgy,[16] which push beyond education by words alone. Others have advocated for the creative use of words through narrative, fiction, and film that integrate emotion, imagination, life experience, and critical reflection on Christian life.[17]

In religious education, there continues to be longing for openness to God's new creation shining through, transforming faith. We still experience tension between a schooling model of education and more creative, holistic ways of forming Christians. Alternatives to a schooling model of education have yet to be given full flesh. Nurturing such alternatives is what this book is about.

A PRACTICAL THEOLOGICAL PROJECT IN CHRISTIAN RELIGIOUS EDUCATION

This book is a practical theological project in Christian religious education that uses the notion of playing to better understand teaching and learning.[18] In this sense, I share affinities with other practical theologians who have addressed issues in their sub-disciplines by drawing on the notion of play.[19] I situate my work in religious education—systems of education that cultivate habits and "dispositions"[20] that draw on sacred wisdom to liberate, heal, and bind together individuals and communities. My own frame of reference is Christian tradition.

This book reflects critically on revelatory experiencing through the language and pedagogies of playing. While individuals can play alone, my

14. Durka and Smith, *Aesthetic Dimensions*. Also Harris, *Teaching and Religious Imagination*.

15. Turpin, *Branded*, 62.

16. Anderson, "Liturgical Catechesis," 349–362; "Worship," 21–32.

17. Seymour et al., "Fiction as Truth," 277–391. See also Roebben, *Seeking Sense in the City*.

18. This book is not a practical theology of play, in which one might expect to explore play as a universal category of human experience.

19. For a literature review of play in relation to practical theological sub-disciplines, see Hamman, "Playing," 47–49.

20. Bourdieu, *Outline*.

focus is on playing together for the sake of being formed in faith. I am interested primarily in playing as it relates to adult learning. In my own mind, pedagogies in adult education are ways of facilitating processes of formation and transformation, of learning and unlearning.

This book makes contributions to at least three areas of scholarly work that have pushed the field of religious education beyond didactic modes of teaching and learning toward creative, experiential formation in Christian faith. First, this work builds on discussions that advocate for religious education as playing, including those of George Albert Coe,[21] David Elkin,[22] and Jerome Berryman.[23] Recognizing the relational character of play, Berryman has inspired widespread use of the Godly Play curriculum. He offers a model for children (and adults playing with children) to experience authenticity and creativity in playing. Drawing on D.W. Winnicott's notion of true self, he argues that playing (i.e., Godly play) is a way of "be[ing] not only with the true self but also with the true self of others."[24] This book expands the notion of playing to include adult Christian formation and draws more deeply from Winnicott and theorists who have been influenced by his work. Second, this work adds to multiple generations of conversations about aesthetic approaches to religious education, which recognize the revelatory power of the arts and their pedagogic implications.[25] It argues that playing for the sake of faith can be more fully understood by taking aesthetic sensibilities into consideration. Third, this volume builds on scholarly work on creative imagination in religious education.[26] It explores anew the ongoing question in the field of how to evoke creative imagination in order to deepen faith.

21. Coe, "Philosophy of Play," 220–22.

22. Elkin, "Role of Play," 282–93.

23. Berryman, *Godly Play*.

24. Ibid., 11.

25. Durka and Smith, *Aesthetic Dimensions*; Lealman and Robinson, *Image of Life*; Westerhoff, "Zion," 5–15; Griffith, "Aesthetical Musings," 16–26; Lealman, "Blue Wind," 74–84; Harris, *Teaching and Religious Imagination*; Goldberg, "Creative Arts Approach," 175–84; Smith, "Table," 301–5; Javore, "Rising from the Ashes."

26. Coe, *What is Christian Education?*; Coe, "Philosophy of Play"; Robinson, "Enfleshing the Word," 356–71; Slee, "'Heaven in Ordinarie,'" 38–57; Moore, *Teaching as a Sacramental Act*; Brelsford, "Schooling Model"; Foster, *Educating Clergy*; Brelsford, "Mythical Realist Orientation," 264–78; Rogers, *Graffiti*; Foster, *From Generation to Generation*.

In exploring the notion of Christians playing, I engage in practical theological method. Practical theology is critical reflection that places experiences, lived assumptions, and actions in dialogue with religious belief, tradition, and practice for the sake of transformation.[27] My hope is that the dialogue is "mutually enriching, intellectually critical, and practically transforming."[28] I follow a long tradition in religious education of turning to the social sciences, particularly psychology, to inform understanding and practice. However, I am perhaps less like an earlier generation of theorists, including Coe, who took more interest in human experience and less interest in divine revelation.[29] Instead I follow the example of other religious educators such as Harrison Elliot, Gabriel Moran, and Maria Harris who have taken seriously the role of revelation as integral to religious education, while still accounting for human experiencing.[30] In exploring invitations to revelatory experiencing in light of playing, my hope is to balance the documentation of human experiencing with critical discussion of theory from theology, social sciences, and theological aesthetics.

The Grace of Playing is a conversation written by a Protestant primarily for theorists, students, and practitioners who are liberal mainline Protestants. Roman Catholic, Orthodox, and Charismatic Christians might be interested in the conversation because the notion of playing helps to illumine what is created in revelatory experiencing, which is traditionally understood in theological terms. However, the view of religious education that this volume presents addresses the problem of inviting revelatory experiencing as encountered in mainline Protestant churches in the United States, which have contextualized theological perspectives on revelation, playing, and aesthetics. At times I refer to "faith communities" with diverse religious traditions in mind. However, it will be up to readers of diverse faith traditions to decide what is useful as they overhear this conversation on Christian religious education.

27. Woodward and Pattison, "Introduction," 7.

28. Ibid.

29. Boys, *Educating in Faith*, 56–57.

30. Elliott, *Religious Education*; Moran, *Theology of Revelation*; *Catechesis of Revelation*; "Revelation as Teaching-Learning"; "Dialogue"; Moran and Harris, *Experiences in Community*.

GRATITUDE FOR GRACE

I have come to know the grace of playing while writing this book, and I did not come to know this by playing alone. *The Grace of Playing* (or "*Grace*" as I have come to know her) has been birthed like any other child—in playing (and laboring) with supportive colleagues, friends, students, family, and community members. When *Grace* existed in the form of ethnographic case studies, Theodore Brelsford, Don Saliers, and Mary Elizabeth Moore were pivotal in helping me wrestle with the implications of voluminous fieldwork. Robyn Neville introduced me to the history of the Rheinland nuns.[31] Pastors (past and present) and members of the Sacramento Japanese United Methodist Church generously agreed to be interviewed. Gary Barbaree, who led a clown troupe at this church when I was a young person, made a deep impression on me about playing and religious education. The co-founders of InterPlay, Cynthia Winton-Henry and Phil Porter, taught me about teaching through play, which has influenced my pedagogy and teaching philosophy. They taught me to associate grace with playing. Members of the InterPlay community, including Masankho Banda, shared deeply from their experiences of the practice. Though *Grace* includes little evidence of ethnographic data, my early work with these individuals and communities formed my thinking and teaching about revelatory experiencing, playing, and aesthetics.

As *Grace* evolved to her current form, I became indebted to another set of supporters. Thanks to Jack Seymour, Dean Blevins, and Elizabeth Caldwell, co-chairs of the HORIZONS in RELIGIOUS EDUCATION Series, and to other colleagues on the editorial review board. I am grateful for the excellent editorial guidance of Ulrike Guthrie, who helped bring *Grace* to final publication. I owe thanks to Carey Newman, who helped me make some key editorial decisions that shaped the scope and trajectory of the manuscript. I am grateful to colleagues Dana Robert, Susanna Snyder, Claire Wolfteich, and Walter Fluker, who provided feedback on chapters. Mary Elizabeth Moore has provided wise counsel, encouragement, and funding to support the research, writing, and publication of *Grace*. I also appreciate the support of the Center for Practical Theology and the faculty of the Boston University School of Theology, which created opportunities for colleagues to engage my work. I am thankful for my graduate research

---

31. In the fourteenth century, nuns in the Rheinland, Germany practiced reverence toward the Christ child and Mary by caring for devotional dolls. I discuss this in terms of playing in chapter 4.

assistants Marc Lavallee, Anna Rozonoer, Margaret Elizabeth Spaulding, Tara Soughers, and Sang-il Kim, who were diligent and responsive to my many requests. Thank God for Barb Kenley who believed in the hope of *Grace* from the very start. I owe gratitude to Laura Ruth Jarrett who created space and hospitality for playing at Hope Central Church in Jamaica Plain.

I am most grateful to a small number of angels and family members who helped me to bring *Grace* into the world. "Mama" Gayle Lenora Stanton gave me a prophetic word about the inner work I needed to do to make way for the "babies" I would birth from my heart. Chris Schlauch has been a dedicated conversation partner. In our playing with ideas, I came to know revelatory experiencing in what Winnicott calls "living an experience together."[32] I am deeply grateful for his incisive feedback, generous support, and expertise on Winnicott. In addition, I am thankful for my loving parents. My father, Leo Goto, passed away before he witnessed the birth of *Grace*, his first "grandchild," but his love of education is written in these pages. My mother, Naomi Goto, created art that became occasions for me to find my voice and to play with others as I reflected on aesthetics, faith, and culture. In writing *Grace*, I have come to receive grace, to make grace with others, and to be transformed by the experience of it.

32. Winnicott theorized that mother and child are able to play when they are "living an experience together," which for him epitomizes the intimate bond that allows both to be creative and spontaneous in one another's company. I address this notion more fully in chapter 5.

chapter 1

INTRODUCTION

When God's new creation shines through moments of teaching and learning, participants in a learning community experience a shift in awareness that draws them in and allows them to perceive what had until then been imperceptible. At a conference, an improvisational theater troupe listens to a man in the audience who shares his story of the truth and reconciliation process in South Africa.[1] The group dramatizes the story for the teller in a moving performance of empathy, which feels poignant and powerful. Other revelatory experiencing unfolds in a seminary classroom, where students sculpt God images from clay and share what they mean in the context of their lives. A student remarks that it "felt like we were doing church." Different revelatory experiencing emerges in the midst of a gospel concert, where the Holy Spirit moves both singers and congregants. People clap, dance, and sing with hearts made open, glad, and alive through praise.

In all of these instances, one might ask what is going on, why experiencing is revelatory one time but not another, and what the resemblances are between these examples. One wonders how to account for what is happening in different contexts, at different times, and in different ways. One might begin to ask what we might do to facilitate this kind of breakthrough learning rather than hoping and waiting for it to occur.

Ethnographic research of communities playing within and beyond the church provoked my own pondering about these questions. In one case, I began to re-see practices of the Japanese American church of my childhood in light of another case study—a community of adults, who engage

---

1. For a description of this performance at the 2007 Religious Education Association annual meeting, see Illman and Smith, *Theology of the Arts*, 110–24.

in InterPlay. Teaching people improvisational techniques of dance, theater, and vocal music, InterPlay is an organization, educational philosophy, and a technique that encourages spontaneous artistic expressions of what feels true in the moment. InterPlay is a spiritual but not religious community; some engage InterPlay as a spiritual practice, others as a life practice.

While I was engaged in fieldwork, I did not have as much theoretical language for what I was observing and participating in as I do now. My early work was focused on thick descriptions of my case studies. *The Grace of Playing* grew out of a need to understand my fieldwork in psychoanalytic, theological, historical, and aesthetic terms. When I began writing, I intended to include full ethnographic studies to reflect my research method as a practical theologian. I could not have written this book without my fieldwork and critical reflection on it. However, in the process of writing I discovered that the subject of playing requires more rigorous, methodical theorizing about playing than I had anticipated. I discuss examples from the case studies in the latter part of the book, but the major work of this volume is about developing analytic tools for excavating those case studies through multiple perspectives of playing. The real project has been to clarify what I mean by revelatory experiencing, why a discussion of playing leads us to deeper understanding of creating conditions for revelatory experiencing, and why religious education needs this. With the theoretical groundwork laid in this book, I can imagine the reader being prepared to delve into ethnographic case studies of communities playing for the sake of faith. However, case studies must be saved for another book.

Curtis Thompson has used the metaphor of translucence to describe how encounters with art can mediate experiences of the holy;[2] the same analogy can be used to describe profound experiencing in religious education. These are times when an everyday instance of religious education becomes "thinner" or translucent, allowing the divine mystery to be seen and felt shining through the experience of being together. It can happen in the context of liturgy, Bible study, serving others, or the many other forms that religious education take. Not all the time, but once in a while learners and teachers register "something more." That experience often prompts one to be with others in new ways, leaving them unexpectedly changed.[3] The experience of this "something more" prompts a different kind of learning than memorizing facts, performing rote actions, or making calculations.

2. Thompson, "Translucence," 3.

3. James, *Varieties of Religious Experience.*

Revelatory experiencing is more personal, compelling, and uncanny than other learning. It often addresses what is needed in the moment for more abundant living and what cannot be sought directly because it was not previously known. Revelatory experiencing feels both full of grace and given by grace. It feels as if God is addressing learners individually as well as collectively. There is conscious recognition of grace in our midst because we receive what is life-giving even when we are unaware of the seeking. Participants often feel bound together by this unexpected gift. Not only have they shared a momentous way of being that is difficult to describe to those who were not present, they sense that it was facilitated in part by being together in ways that cannot be replicated. In short, human beings hunger for revelatory experiencing because it is of God, it calls deeply to us, and it summons to awareness what is usually unrecognized. Yet revelatory experiencing can neither be predicted nor demanded.

Revelatory experiencing causes in learners a destabilizing and re-orienting shift in awareness or feeling that allows them to encounter divine mystery, themselves, and others in new, life-giving ways. Revelatory experiencing presupposes practices that decenter habitual patterns of thinking, feeling, and doing, both individually and together, which opens up possibilities for re-centering. Decentering and re-centering are not simply done *to* learners but *with* them. The relationships that are formed and sustained in revelatory experiencing allow learners to participate in the unfolding of the learning process. Learners are not simply given what is needed; they contribute to a process that precipitates the creative emergence of something of God that needs to be perceived.

A theoretical challenge for understanding revelatory experiencing is that there are neither precise nor accurate words to concretize or hold it up for examination. In fact, the more one attempts to parse what is going on in revelatory experiencing, the more the embodied memory and wonder of translucence seems to dissipate. While theoretical discussions thrive on specificity and sharpness, any description of revelatory experiencing is inherently vague, like telling someone who has never seen snow what it is like to ski. One can only grasp experience by analogy and association, by aiming as close as possible in words, knowing that the words do not land solidly or precisely on target.

I use the language of *revelatory experiencing* rather than *revelatory experiences* with some intention. Revelatory experiences suggest peak or prized events or states of being that should be sought because they are intrinsically rewarding. There is a danger of approaching revelatory experiences as if they were something to *have* and assuming that the more experiences one accumulates the better. Instead, the notion of revelatory experiencing is meant to convey a *process* of living into deeper and more authentic ways of being and being with one another. Instead of "having" a certain kind of experience happen to me, my being and being with others and Spirit is an open-ended process that involves invitation and participation.

A primary task of religious education is to help form and transform people to create a more just and peaceful world. This is what grounds my understanding of revelatory experiencing. In particular, I understand Christian religious education to be systems that cultivate habits and dispositions that align with the ways of Jesus—ways that liberate, heal, and bind together individuals and communities. Gabriel Moran and Maria Harris call this "teaching the way,"[4] and Jack Seymour entitles his volume on Christian education *Teaching the Way of Jesus*.[5] However, as a Japanese American practical theologian, I am sensitive to there being multiple ways of understanding Jesus' life and teachings and numerous ways of practicing Christian faith. Practices of faith are essential to forming habits and "dispositions"[6] that characterize Christian living appropriate to a particular context. Practices of religious education shape the faithful both formally, informally, intentionally, unintentionally, and by their absence.[7]

FROM REVELATION TO REVELATORY EXPERIENCING

Though related to revelation, revelatory experiencing is its own phenomenon. The two differ from one another primarily in magnitude rather than in substance. Revelatory experiencing is distinguishable from divine revelation, which is "the illumination of all creation which still lives partially in darkness awaiting the birth of a new creation."[8] Revelatory experiencing is also distinct from Christian revelation, in which divine revelation takes form in the person of Jesus Christ, whose life becomes the lens through which to understand a pattern of divine revelation in the history of God's people before and after Jesus' life and death. In revelatory experiencing,

4. Harris and Moran, *Reshaping Religious Education*, 36, 44–55.

5. Seymour, *Teaching the Way*.

6. Bourdieu, *Outline*.

7. Eisner, *Educational Imagination*.

8. Moran, "Dialogue," 42.

some of what transforms human thinking, feeling, and doing is both divine revelation and Christian revelation. However, revelatory experiencing involves more modest learning encounters and exists on a continuum with revelation. Revelation in its most exalted form happens to someone, as in Paul's experience on the road to Damascus. The focus in revelation is on God's salvific action in which God acts as the agent, even though revelation remains a human experience. In contrast, revelatory experiencing draws attention to the human role in preparing for, receiving, and participating in processes of Spirit. While revelations can speak to or have significance for the whole of humanity for all time, revelatory experiencing intimately involves particular learners in a particular time and place. These ordinary awakenings are less intense than those at the other end of the spectrum, but they help to nurture habits and dispositions that characterize (in this case) Christian living nonetheless.

Revelatory experiencing is related to revelation, but not as revelation is traditionally understood. In some traditions, revelation is an "authoritative deposit of truth, usually in propositional form."[9] For example, Protestant evangelicals might appeal to the saving truth of the Gospel, which must be spread throughout all people, while Roman Catholics give credence to tradition and the magisterium.[10] Conservative approaches to revelation within these traditions tend to lead to transmissive pedagogies in religious education.[11] While these might be valuable in ensuring the continuity of Christian revelation, excessive use of transmissive teaching methods can be experienced as rigid, domineering, and impersonal. Of course, good pedagogy—conservative or liberal—can include moments of transmissive teaching; it's a matter of proportion.

Revelatory experiencing is related to revelation but understood in a more theologically liberal vein. Rather than approaching Christian revelation as a totalizing "meta-narrative" and determining revelation on the basis of content, theological liberals tend to view revelation as a certain kind of experience precipitated by the Bible and/or tradition.[12] Such assumptions about revelation lead theological liberals (including me) to prefer

---

9. Heywood, *Divine Revelation*, 171.

10. Ibid.

11. Ibid., 3, 171. In a transmissive mode of teaching, the instructor engages in a one-way, linguistic transfer of knowledge, much like a radio broadcast. Brelsford, "Three Modes."

12. Heywood, *Divine Revelation*, 3, 171; Astley, "On Learning Religion," 32.

experiential modes of teaching and learning.[13] I share the assumption that an aim of Christian religious education is "to provide the 'paintbox' rather than the full picture, the resources needed to create a coherent Christian faith for the current situation rather than the fully digested wisdom of previous generations."[14]

Revelatory experiencing makes clear the fundamentally relational and social nature of revelation, which happens "in between" persons as they relate to one another.[15] "The reality is the relation; the meeting is the revelation. . . . Persons reveal, and it is the persons who are revealed; through being persons they reveal, and through revealing they become persons."[16] What is being revealed within personal relationships is the embodiment of the gospel as God in our midst is felt, experienced, and believed. As seen on a small scale in revelatory experiencing, revelation implies that Christianity (as a tradition of certain kinds of experiencing together) "is a revelation."[17] Christians are "a community of people engaged in and becoming aware of a disclosure of Being in the present"[18]—being more fully with oneself, with God, and with one another.

THE NEED FOR THE LANGUAGE OF PLAYING

More incisive language is needed to name critically what many religious educators know about creating conditions for revelatory experiencing. An analogy might be how learning Bloom's taxonomy opens up teaching and learning in new, critical ways. A teacher knows much about teaching and learning without knowing Bloom's way of thinking about pedagogy. However, the taxonomy allows the teacher to see the familiar in ways that she might not have recognized previously. Terms of the taxonomy serve as stand-ins that allow a person to visualize what's going on in teaching and learning. In the case of religious education, religious educators need a rich language to identify, refine, and express what they know about facilitating

---

13. Heywood, *Divine Revelation*, 3, 171.

14. Astley, "Tradition and Experience," 42. Cited in Heywood, *Divine Revelation*, 171.

15. Moran and Harris, *Experiences in Community*, 75. Harris, *Teaching and Religious Imagination*, 62; Moran, "Revelation as Teaching-Learning," 278.

16. Moran and Harris, *Experiences in Community*, 75. Harris, *Teaching and Religious Imagination*, 62.

17. Ibid.

18. Ibid.

revelatory experiencing, so that they might build on what they know and to see it anew. Another aim is to help learners to embrace revelatory experiencing more fully by knowing some of the language of playing, so that they too can recognize it when they see it.

To explore revelatory experiencing, one could use the language of "religious experience," "flow experiences," or "aesthetic experience."[19] Alternatively, as this book proposes, one can turn to the language of "playing." Each of these rhetorics has strengths and limitations in opening up revelatory experiencing to greater view. None of these rhetorics land entirely or exactly on revelatory experiencing (just as Bloom's taxonomy does not fully capture all that is involved in teaching and learning). Borrowing terms and concepts from multiple languages can be helpful and inevitable sometimes, especially because there are natural affinities and overlaps between them. However, the language of playing offers some of the most compelling advantages, despite its limitations.

The language of "religious experience" speaks to experiences of transcendence, which are singular and transformational.[20] One could talk of religious experience as a means of understanding some of what happens in revelatory experiencing (e.g., how learners awaken to the divine and other mysteries). However, this would risk conflating religious experience with experiences of revelation or revelatory experiencing, and they are not the same. Experiences of revelation are a kind of religious experience, which is much broader. As William James has made us aware, there are "varieties of religious experience."[21] Neither religious experiences nor experiences of revelation are of the same order as revelatory experiencing, which religious educators manage to facilitate regularly though without certainty of outcomes. Revelatory experiencing might not take place in the context of religion and be experienced as being more spiritual than religious.

The language of "flow" that Mihalyi Csikszentmihalyi uses has its own advantages for opening up the notion of revelatory experiencing. Flow "denotes the wholistic sensation present when we act with total involvement. It is the kind of feeling after which one nostalgically says: 'That was fun,' or 'That was enjoyable.'"[22] This concept is wide-reaching in that flow-producing activities include not only art but religion and play. The language of flow

19. Csikszentmihalyi, *Flow.*

20. Neitz and Spickard, "Steps," 18.

21. James, *Varieties of Religious Experience.*

22. Csikszentmihalyi, "Play and Intrinsic Rewards," 43.

provides a close account for some revelatory experiencing, for example as it occurs sometimes in playing sports.[23] Flow highlights how certain activities can produce pleasant, life-giving experiences of being carried away or utterly absorbed by what one is doing. However, the notion of flow has its limitations for describing revelatory experiencing, because such experiencing is not always fun or entertaining though it is meaningful.[24] Because revelatory experiencing evokes a wide range of emotions, it therefore cannot be reduced to flow.[25] Csikszentmihalyi dismisses theological motivations for engaging in religious practices, arguing that flow is the primary reason most people so engage.[26] Furthermore, the language of flow does not account sufficiently for the relational nature of revelatory experiencing.[27] Flow is an outcome of engaging an activity, not a result of the way in which people relate to one another in the process.

The language of "aesthetic experience" provides more helpful words and concepts to describe what can precipitate experiences of revelation as well as revelatory experiencing. In theological aesthetics, experiences of beauty (along with truth and goodness) have long been understood as what mediates, embodies, and brings human beings closer to the divine. Various art forms allow the holy to be expressed and experienced in different ways.[28] Traditionally, we have understood art that is revelatory as a means to symbolize or image God. We experience revelation in the "assimilation" of art, as human beings take in God's ways of being and give them form in words, images, and other media.[29] This approach accounts well for an active human role in revelation. However, much of the work in theological aesthetics focuses on fine art, which reveals the limitation of drawing on this language for religious education. Even though religious educators facilitate revelatory experiencing both with and without art, the language of aesthetics is vital to understanding revelatory experiencing, which is whole-bodied.

When I use the term *aesthetics*, I refer to "that dealing with sensory perception and rooted in the body," which Alexander Baumgarten calls

---

23. Kelly, "Sport," 169–72.

24. Nietz and Spickard, "Steps," 25–26.

25. Ibid., 27.

26. Ibid., 26.

27. Ibid., 27–28.

28. Van der Leeuw, *Sacred and Profane Beauty*.

29. Viladesau, *Theological Aesthetics*, 94.

"natural aesthetics."[30] Other theorists take a more narrow approach, using the notion of aesthetics to discuss perception, interpretation, and experience of objects or works of art. However, approaching aesthetics as a language for discussing sense perception and bodily experience is grounded in an older understanding of *aisthesis* (Greek for "sensory perception"). In the mid 1700s, Alexander Baumgarten, who gave the modern field of aesthetics its name, focused not on beauty but on sensual knowing.[31] Because religious education in its many forms is not simply cognitive but also affective and sensual, a broader understanding of aesthetics as bodily experience is helpful though incomplete without a theological nuancing. Theological aesthetics, understood as "what moves the human heart,"[32] helps to frame sense perception in terms of spiritual response and formation. Reflecting on what and how sense experiences move people also invites contextual analysis. However, I am cautious about limiting discussion to how a person responds to external sources of beauty, such as a beautiful painting. Instead, I emphasize *relational dynamics* that move the human heart in revelatory experiencing. Hence, I turn to the language of playing, though later I will also retrieve the language of aesthetics to highlight an important perspective on playing.

At first, the language of playing might seem like the least likely of rhetorics to use in exploring revelatory experiencing. With the language of playing comes cultural, theological, and ecclesial baggage that could lend irreverent or other negative connotations to a discussion about revelatory experiencing. In common understanding, playing is associated with fun, frivolity, and childishness. Economic interests reinforce a persistent, distorted, but seductive notion of what playing is. Play (and all the stuff needed to play) has been commodified, packaged, and marketed to appeal to all sectors. Small children beg parents for the hottest toys on the market. Adults horde expensive "toys" (be it clothes, gadgets, or sports memorabilia) that they collect, covet, and play with. The dizzying pace of change, the pressures of living, and constant threats to human wellbeing make consumers vulnerable to the belief that playing is a much-deserved reward or escape for purchase. All of this seems far removed and deeply inimical to revelatory experiencing. This is partly due to a lack of a robust

30. Plate, "Skin of Religion," 167.

31. Ibid., 166

32. García-Rivera, *Community of the Beautiful*, 9.

practical theology of play that offers alternative ways of thinking critically about playing.

Historically Christian traditions have held an ambivalent view of playing. Epitomized in the Protestant work ethic but preceded by Augustine, this view considers the model person to be hard working, frugal, self-reliant, and ambitious.[33] Historically, a person's work is the criterion by which to judge success, while playing is considered time off from work—understood either as "a [mere] reward for past work, a temptation to idleness, or a pause that refreshes."[34] More recently playing has been made more theologically palatable when justified in terms of Sabbath.[35] However, Sabbath-keeping is not widely practiced in Christian communities.[36] The notion of playing can also stir up uneasiness inherited from the Church Fathers, for whom playing comes too close to sensual, worldly pleasures, and sexual titillations. Furthermore, playing raises fears about messing with what is holy. The idea of playing can threaten deeply held beliefs that govern how adult Christians act and how we picture ourselves as church people. It unsettles ecclesial norms about how we express ourselves, what we share, and who is in charge.

The inherent risks of using the language of playing can be tempered by drawing on theoretical understandings that neither come from consumer culture, nor strictly from theology, nor from ecclesial norms. Speaking of playing from theological as well as social scientific perspectives helps to dispel some of the common and historic associations of play, though not entirely. Referring in the same breath to both playing and what is holy may feel threatening or sacrilegious at times because we have deeply internalized distorted notions of playing. However, a book on revelatory experiencing in light of playing is appropriately an imaginative, creative venture that seeks Spirit at the edges of what is accepted in both church and academy.

Despite its potential risks, the language of playing offers an entrance into critical reflection on revelatory experiencing that is true to the relational nature of revelation, which is something other rhetorics lack. While revelation is commonly understood as happening *within* individuals, Moran and Harris locate revelation as taking place in *between* people, because

---

33. Johnston, *Christian at Play*, 85.

34. Ibid.

35. Ibid., 88–95.

36. This was found to be the case in a study of urban pastors. Stone and Wolfteich, *Sabbath in the City*.

"the meeting is the revelation."[37] In agreement with this view, my account of revelatory experiencing suggests that playing can be a theoretical language that explicitly accounts for relational dynamics between participants. Winnicott, a British psychoanalyst and pediatrician, does this particularly well when he focuses on the space between people and what is created when we play together. This psychoanalytic theory describes the human maturation process, which is not completely separate from experiences of revelation (big or small). Revelation, especially in its most mundane forms, is experienced within the "natural processes of human learning,"[38] which include playing. The implication is that the language of playing illumines how human beings anticipate, receive, participate in, and respond to everyday experiences of awakening to divine or other truths. Of course, psychoanalytic theory alone is insufficient for exploring revelatory experiencing because it ignores theological, historic, and aesthetic dimensions Therefore, these other perspectives will also be needed.

Winnicott's language of playing provides critical pushback to thinking of pedagogy as aimed at facilitating individual experience, for that fails to account for the communal, relational nature of Christian formation. By emphasizing the relational character of playing, Winnicott provides insight about revelatory experiencing, not merely because it evokes creativity and imagination but also because people need each other for spiritual growth. This psychoanalytic theory helps to illumine how revelatory experiencing unfolds not only within the individual but also between and among individuals in a community.

One limitation of drawing heavily from object relations theory is that it is derived from a clinical paradigm of working with individuals. In contrast, religious education addresses both individual and communal formation in multiple contexts. There are important differences in discussing children playing versus playing in adulthood, therapy versus faith formation, as well as what happens in the clinic versus church and other contexts. However, understanding the human psyche is essential for Christian formation if it is to liberate, heal, and bind together individuals and communities. Some of the most challenging work of religious education is not only to help the faithful to learn what is godly but also to unlearn patterns that keep them from living fully. For these reasons, psychoanalytic theory is key.

37. See n. 15 above.
38. Heywood, *Divine Revelation*, 168.

The language of playing opens up conversation about pedagogies for "leaning into" God's new creation.[39] Although revelation can be experienced on an individual basis, revelatory experiencing that allows people to lean into God's new creation is communal. God's new creation is something not only to understand in conceptual terms but also to experience with others and with Spirit in order to be formed in Christian faith. The new creation requires Christians to be, to be with others, and to behave in new ways, including those that might challenge habitual ways of being. In this sense, the image of leaning into God's new creation is one of resistance to the status quo and change from old to new. One of the tasks of religious education is to employ various pedagogies that facilitate de-centering and re-centering, allowing learners to tilt toward what cannot be experienced alone and toward what is more life-giving. Learners can lean farther if they are connected to one another, stretching toward God's new creation.

More than ever, Christian communities need revelatory experiencing that reinvigorates faith and investment in the community. In this age of ecclesial transition, ordinary Christians are seeking experiences of Spirit more than apologetics on Christian beliefs.[40] There is a turning away from "rationalism, positivism, materialism, and industrial capitalism . . . to a rediscovery especially of the religious dimension of experience, ethical debates and aesthetical sensibility."[41] Churches have much to offer if they intentionally provide opportunities for playing, where the faithful might have creative encounters with mystery and one another. They could also do a service to the world by facilitating and reflecting theologically on revelatory experiencing beyond church walls, helping others to recognize Spirit creatively partnering everywhere for the sake of the new creation.

SEEKING THE GRACE OF PLAYING

The thesis of this book is that creating conditions for revelatory experiencing can be better understood in light of playing. Put another way, the notion of playing provides insights into pedagogies in which learners are creating and are created anew. One premise of this argument is that one need not wait for revelation to dawn or to fall from the sky. Rather, one can wisely shape pedagogies of playing that invite and prepare the faithful to welcome,

39. Guttesen, *Leaning*; Hauerwas and Willimon, *Lord, Teach Us.*

40. Cox, *Future of Faith.*

41. Gräb, "Church, Religion," 88.

experience, and fully participate in translucence. A second premise of this work is that revelatory experiencing "hits home" according to who learners are, what their needs are in the moment, and where they are in a time and place. What works on one occasion will not necessarily work in another. What can be more effective in one community might be less so in another. Facilitating revelatory experiencing requires becoming increasingly astute at imagining case by case the most conducive conditions for learners. A third premise is that living in a world of rapid change and institutional transition constantly keeps us reeling. We need experiences that interrupt what keeps us off-kilter, so that we can re-center ourselves.

I devote the first part of the book to exploring the complexity of playing in relation to revelatory experiencing, establishing theoretical frameworks, and lending a historical point of reference. In the second and third chapters, I situate playing in relation to psychoanalytic and theological approaches, which become lenses for engaging historical examples in the fourth chapter. Psychoanalytic and theological concepts help to open up medieval practices of holy fools playing by pretense and nuns playing with devotional dolls, as well as contemporary practices of devotion toward the Infant of Prague. The examples offer insights for which theory has yet to account. In the fifth chapter, I re-evaluate the grounds for playing. I provide additional analytic concepts from an aesthetic perspective that illumine the spaces, conditions, and dynamics for playing. I introduce the term *local practical theological aesthetics* to help readers consider how their particular religious community plays according to contextually sensitive, aesthetic sensibilities that are conducive to revelatory experiencing. The final chapter gathers together insights for playing and God's new creation, broadening a vision for playing within and beyond ecclesial institutions.

chapter 2

PLAYING SOCIAL SCIENTIFICALLY: THE MEANINGS OF PLAYING

If the language of playing can elucidate what it means to invite revelatory experiencing, pinning down what playing is would seem to be the next task. Theorists often depend on definitions as anchoring points of reference and as stimuli for debate. However, defining assumes that with increasing degrees of accuracy one can articulate the objective essence of a word so that its definition is universally true. Like many other forms of human experiencing (e.g., love), playing defies definition because one cannot easily encapsulate the essence of playing (if there is such a thing). Furthermore, one cannot divorce one's subjectivity in order to make sense of a term. Playing is mostly grasped by way of experience, with each person bringing various experiences of playing to comprehending what playing means. More careful use of the term *experiencing* is needed to make clear the roles of feeling and conceptualizing in the process of making the term *playing* meaningful.

In general, experiencing involves noticing or what Eugene Gendlin calls "inward attending" to the "flow of feeling" that shapes one's inner sense.[1] Experiencing is "pre-conceptual"—what is lived before words come to mind.[2] The flow of feeling can involve sensing emotions, including strong emotions. However, in Gendlin's understanding, the content of what is felt is not as important as attending to inner states moment by moment. Feeling is not a "chaotic mass to be avoided" or tamed by logic and discursive

1. Gendlin, *Experiencing*, 11–12.
2. Ibid., 10.

thinking[3]; however, neither feeling nor logic alone can provide meaning. "Meaning is formed in the interaction of experiencing and something that functions symbolically. Feeling without symbolization is blind; symbolization without feeling is empty."[4] In this case, I am using "playing" as a "verbal symbol" to open up the reader's memory of what is familiar.

Attempting to define playing in essential terms might not be as helpful as characterizing it, which leaves room for multiple felt senses of playing to engage concepts that are offered. In other words, conveying the meanings of playing also involves evoking memories of playing, which requires description and characterization. Only then do the words (as symbolizations of playing) join with the embodied memories of playing. I am deliberately referring to "playing" rather than "play" to emphasize the experience rather than to simply identify a category of human behavior that can be parsed.

Ironically, grasping the experience of playing does not lay bare the felt sense of revelatory experiencing, as if doing so fully unveils the latter. This would assume that playing and revelatory experiencing are coterminous, which they are not. What we have are two verbal symbols—playing and revelatory experiencing—each of which corresponds to processes in the vicinity of one another. In this book, I use the term *revelatory experiencing* as a symbol for the felt sense of gracious awakening, opening, and relating deeply to others. Another way of symbolizing some of these felt senses is playing. The symbol "playing" has the advantage of being widely researched from multiple social scientific as well as theological perspectives. Religious educators may recognize revelatory experiencing in their pedagogy more easily than playing because the connection with revelation is more apparent. However, some of the terms and concepts related to playing can illumine more richly some of the felt senses to which playing and revelatory experiencing point.

A CHARACTERIZATION OF PLAYING

To play is to experience losing and finding oneself in engaging reality and one another "as if," exploring freely a world of possibilities bounded by structure that facilitates relationship. This is a descriptive approach to convey the meanings of playing. This characterization offers multiple terms, stimulating experiential memories that enrich the meanings of the symbol *playing*.

3. Ibid., 8.
4. Ibid., 5, 8.

First, the notion "losing and finding" oneself is important to the mean-ings of playing by bringing to mind a familiar experience. When a child be-comes "lost" in a game of pretend or when an adult becomes engrossed in watching a film, the person has been decentered from life as usual. It is only upon emerging from a play world that a person registers a difference—of having been somewhere else. A player can lose herself in the experience of playing, yet strangely she can emerge with a sense of being "found." Upon reflection, a player might conclude: "When I am playing, I feel most like myself," or "I have felt something of God." In these instances, something hidden comes to light. Sometimes the possibilities of a pretend world or a filmic world, for example, are made meaningful as they correspond to the player's life, creating an opportunity for re-centering. Some thinkers have noted the possibility of experiencing transcendence while playing, in the sense of finding oneself in the midst of something larger than oneself.[5]

Acting "as if" similarly lends meaning to playing. Playing allows a person to sense what is authentic or real by inviting the player to enter a fictive world. Acting or believing "as if" entails setting aside enough disbelief, appearances, or literal ways of thinking to shift temporarily into another way of engaging reality and one another.[6] Rooted in the Greek verb *prospoieomai*, which means "to pretend," playing involves a *poietic* world characterized not only by make-believe, but of acting or believing "as if" certain everyday ways of being in the world were suspended.[7] Playing "as if" is commonplace: male friends fight "as if" they were going to hurt one another; readers believe "as if" when they enter the fictional world of a novel; and a child plays with a cardboard box "as if" it were a house. Even in conversation, two colleagues can be so engrossed that they act "as if" noth-ing else exists but the world they are spinning out. Possibilities abound. Alternative realities can be inhabited, explored, and abandoned. When playing becomes encompassing or compelling, players can be moved intel-lectually and emotionally, and be touched spiritually. Not only are the effects of playing real, sometimes a player feels sorry when playing ends because he/she has experienced something real while playing "as if." One might think that "pretending" is related to falsification, but in fact sometimes the

---

5. See Ackerman, *Deep Play*; Kelly, *Sport*, 163–77.

6. Singer and Singer, *House of Make-Believe*; Apter, "Structural-Phenomenology," 13–30; Kerr, "Structural-Phenomenology," 31–42; Volkwein, "Play as a Path," 359–70.

7. Miller, *Gods and Games*, 143.

make-believe involved in playing has more to do with authentication or approaching that which is more real.[8]

The notion of "as if" has a long basis in philosophical, literary, and psychoanalytic traditions, made well known by Hans Vaihinger, who wrote *The Philosophy of "As If."*[9] Vaihinger argues that fictive thinking gives rise to scholarly work in diverse fields, including mathematics, the sciences, law, philosophy, literature, and theology. He surmises that at the heart of fictive thinking in all of these fields is willingness to consider an impossible or un-real condition in theorizing about the unknown. Vaihinger's notion of "as if" can be traced to the way fiction (and, I infer, fictive thinking) had been approached in empirical philosophy, specifically to Francis Bacon, who condemned idols as fiction, and Jeremy Bentham, who understood fiction as inevitable and productive in scholarly thinking.[10] Nietzsche influenced Vaihinger's thinking, "especially . . . [his] early essay 'On Truth and Lies in a Non-Moral Sense' ('nonmoral lying' is understood to be 'the conscious de-viation from reality to be found in myth, art, metaphor, etc.') and *The Birth of Tragedy* ('art is the conscious creation of an aesthetic illusion')."[11] One can recognize Nietzsche's thinking when Vaihinger argues that, "life and science are not possible without imaginary, therefore false conceptions."[12]

Related to fictive thinking, the notion of a "world of possibilities" is a third key term for grasping the meanings of playing. The possibilities of playing may be concrete—as in winning a point or hitting a home run—or they may be ephemeral, fleeting, and imaginary. In this latter sense, play-ing ignites the senses and imagination as possibilities emerge, fall away, are reborn, and change—sometimes quixotically moment by moment, other times with subtlety, strategy, or deliberation. To be swept up in this swirl-ing, hurtling dance of possibilities can be life giving, deepening, and some-times challenging. Creative possibilities are generative, unfolding more and more.

While playing alone can be absorbing, transporting, and fulfilling, playing together multiplies possibilities as creative ideas, resources, and energies collide, compete, resonate, or are amplified. Playing together can

---

8. Informal conversation with Stanford Goto.

9. Vaihinger, *Philosophy of 'As If'*.

10. Stampfl, "Ghostly Presence," 439. Iser, *Fictive and the Imaginary*, 108. For Ben-them, see ibid., 112, 119.

11. Miklowitz, *Metaphysics to Metafictions*, xxiv.

12. Ibid.

extend a sense of agency in players as they participate in, construct, and are shaped by possibilities. Members of a basketball team play out the possibilities of the game. In singing together people experience something more than singing alone, with more possibilities to match with others or to sense one's distinctiveness by contrast. Playing with others creates more possibilities for inspiration, action, and response as players make their own contributions. What players are doing is less important than what they are registering—a heightened awareness of what is emerging, an expansive freedom that is energizing, and an excitement for participating in what could not be created alone.[13] "Losing oneself," entering a "world of possibilities," and acting "as if" together form a network of terms that indicate what is meant by *playing*. However, they also comprise a network of practices that imparts meaning through the doing of them.

Along with "losing oneself," entering a "world of possibilities," and acting "as if," there are other practices inherent in playing. First, playing is grounded in the practice of being creative, using one's imagination and other resources to do so. When a person re-imagines in order to see things anew, it generates fresh possibilities as a person brings the sharp edge of creativity to carve up, rearrange, and add to what is familiar in arresting ways. Second, playing involves the practice of abiding by the structures of playing, which are given to or created by the players themselves.[14] Structures help to sustain and guide playing, by providing a sense of one or another "world" in which a person may play—where it begins and ends, what holds true and what does not, as well as who is playing and who is not. Third, playing together includes the practice of sensing and responding to other players, which builds a sense of community.[15] Players are bound by the same structures, space, and culture of the play world, which mediate the emerging dynamics between and among participants as they venture together. Playing with the same people is never the same twice, and playing with different players is new every time.

Fourth, playing involves the practice of being open to surprise and wonder, cultivating this as a habit in participants.[16] As *poiesis*, playing brings into existence something that has not existed before. Players often

13. Kaufman, *In Face of Mystery*, 277.

14. Huizinga, *Homo Ludens*; Berryman, *Godly Play*; Koppel, *Open-Hearted Ministry*; and Evans, *Playing*.

15. Huizinga, *Homo Ludens*, 7–13; Johnston, *Christian at Play* 35, 40–41.

16. Neale, *In Praise of Play*, 166; Keen, *Apology for Wonder*, 27–28.

surprise each other with unpredictable moves; a performer surprises an audience; participants discover or create newness that changes the course of their playing. Sometimes surprise is accompanied by delight, but even when a surprise is disturbing, frightening, or disorienting, a player learns to adapt or hold it lightly to sustain the playing. Some people argue that the moment that playing turns unpleasant it becomes something other than playing, especially in the case of children.[17] However, many adults appreciate a wider experience of playing and a fuller range of emotions that can make experiences of playing powerful, compelling, and ineffable. Some players develop a tolerance or even a taste for feeling disoriented in playing. For example, some people love roller coasters or movies that frighten the viewer. Sometimes a surprise that disturbs can provoke fascination, curiosity, or deeper attention. From a learning standpoint, surprise can be a powerful pedagogy.

Playing involves and encourages the practice of wonder. Wonder is "feeling excited by an encounter with something novel and unexpected, something that strikes a person as intensely real, true, or beautiful."[18] Experiences of wonder provoke a sudden "decentering of the self" and invite a "recentering."[19] Playing can feel deep, dramatic, or overwhelming when a person is grasped by wonder—the same feeling as when a person encounters the mystery of God. It makes a person sit up and take notice because habitual patterns of thinking, feeling, and doing have been suddenly jostled. Experiences of wonder trigger not an analytic parsing of parts but contemplation of how parts relate to an unseen whole.[20] They inspire a person to consider creative possibilities, to construct plausible explanations for being taken by surprise perceptions.[21]

The language of playing offers new insights about revelatory experiencing, which might not be accessed best by using theological language alone. First, the notion of losing and finding oneself calls attention to how revelatory experiencing unveils an unexpected gift even though it was not sought directly. Second, the notion of playing "as if" brings clarity to how believers live into the newness of expanding faith. In playing "as if" God's new creation were already here, Christians trust enough to suspend normal

17. Eberle "Edge of Play," 168, 173–74.
18. Bulkeley, *Wondering Brain*, 3.
19. Ibid., 4.
20. Fuller, *Wonder*, 8–9.
21. Ibid., 86.

or routine ways of being in the world, opening up what is more gracious or needed in the moment. This will be discussed more fully later in this chapter. Third, the notion of entering a world of possibilities is another way of understanding the way that life breaks open in revelatory experiencing. Fourth, the fact that playing invites creativity and imagination reminds us of our being made in God's image. As discussed in the next chapter, creativity is the Spirit's transformative movement in the world, from which human creativity draws. This is why revelatory experiencing and playing foster human awakening. Fifth, the fact that playing happens powerfully between and among people points to the relational nature of revelatory experiencing. Sixth, the notion that playing invites a person to be open to being surprised suggests that Christians are to anticipate revelatory experiencing, not knowing when and where encounters with mystery will arise. The biblical text is full of events, reversals, and twists that are intended to take the faithful by surprise and inspire re-examination and fresh approaches. In turn, the faithful must learn to "expect the unexpected" as part of Christian life.[22]

Finally, the notion of practicing wonder in playing reveals some of what is lived in revelatory experiencing, as it involves complex emotions of puzzlement, ambivalence, and/or admiration.[23] When an object of wonder disturbs one's preconceived categories, such moments can be holy. They can be revelatory if one allows the object to "speak" for itself as a "Thou" rather than an "It."[24] Such moments can be formative in that they impart humility, as a player holds back from imposing categories on the other, including objects and people.[25] With practice, a person is able to encounter an other (even a familiar one) as if for the first time, allowing for an experience of wonder. In playing, experiences of wonder train the senses to catch a fleeting hold of God's mystery in surprising forms, to pause in the presence of it, and to ponder it gently and reverently.[26] One cannot help but be de-centered and re-centered toward God as a result of playing.

Naturally, in presenting a characterization of playing as it relates to revelatory experiencing, I have left out a common way to describe playing.

22. Moore, *Teaching as a Sacramental Act.*

23. Keen, *Apology for Wonder,* 27–29.

24. Ibid., 26, 34.

25. Ibid., 26–27.

26. Ibid. Also Harris, *Teaching and Religious Imagination,* 21; Zajonc, "Cognitive-Affective Connections," 3.

Many play theorists argue that playing is for the sake of enjoyment and is intrinsically motivated.[27] One could posit that children jump rope for the sake of experiencing the joy of the activity itself, and for no other purpose. This line of thinking approaches playing as an activity whose intrinsic goods are limited to that particular activity. However, I am approaching playing as a form of engaging reality and one another that can be lived in many instances and through diverse activities, including those that one might not commonly think of as playing. Unlike jumping rope, revelatory experiencing cannot be equated or reduced to activities per se, though it can be facilitated by one or another activity. I am also interested in exploring what playing creates for the player and what playing creates between and among the players, neither of which implies an instrumental view of playing. One can ask what jumping rope creates for the player, even if the practice is engaged for its own sake. Likewise, one can ponder what would make the jumping experience even better. By extension, I believe the faithful can experience in worship what can be described as playing even though they are engaged in worship for its own sake.

MANY APPROACHES TO PLAYING AND LEARNING

Focusing on approaches to playing and learning, particularly from the perspective of outcomes, is helpful because learning is involved in revelatory experiencing. Much of the literature about what is learned by playing pertains to children but is also useful for thinking about playing into adulthood, especially as it relates to religious education. Three perspectives assist in setting the stage to make comparisons and contrasts with Winnicott's approach to playing.[28]

First, "escapist" perspectives on playing assume that playing is a human activity that results in nothing being learned. Understood mainly in terms of leisure, playing is "surplus energy, relaxation, recreation, or catharsis."[29] Playing provides escape; it has nothing to do with reality. Among classic play theorists such as Johan Huizinga and Roger Callois, play is characterized in stark opposition to the so-called "real world."[30] Playing is understood

27. Apter, "Structural-Phenomenology," 13–30; Caillois, *Les Jeux et les Hommes*; Huizinga, *Homo Ludens*; Kraus, *Recreation and Leisure*.

28. Sutton-Smith, *Play and Learning*, 314–15.

29. Ibid., 314.

30. Ehrmann, et al., "Homo Ludens Revisited," 31–57.

as non-productive and engaged for its own sake, whereas what happens in the "real world" is considered utilitarian and serious. In contrast with work, playing is thought to exist in a bubble, somehow free and untouched by reality.[31] If it were more serious, playing would be too productive and would therefore no longer constitute playing.

"Escapist" approaches to playing fail to shed light on revelatory experiencing because they presume that one disconnects from reality in order to play, avoiding what there is to know in reality. By this understanding, one could not experience what is revelatory in the play world. If revelatory experiencing involves an unveiling of mystery, which enriches human understanding so that reality can be engaged more fully, then there is no place for revelatory experiencing in playing (in the escapist sense).

There are significant problems with assuming that playing is disconnected from reality. It assumes that all reality is given, objectively knowable, and universally understood, as if the "real world" were obvious. In this way of thinking, if one is not playing, then by default one is experiencing reality as it "really is." While the tendency is to take perception as reality without a second thought, many aspects of reality are too big, too unpredictable, or too complex for the human mind to grasp. There are also dimensions of reality that human beings keep from consciously knowing or accepting. Some truths are too scary or overwhelming; therefore human beings avoid confronting reality head on. What remains a mystery can only be approached in mediated form through games,[32] metaphor,[33] ritual,[34] festival,[35] poetics,[36] or the subjunctive mood—through playing, as it were.

Treating play as if it were separable from reality implies that playing is a luxury that those in the "real world" can only enjoy when they can. However, playing is critical even in places where one would think the reality of poverty, injustice, or other forms of oppression would stamp out playing. Human beings still play as a liberative means of coming to know what is life-giving. Even in the midst of slavery, African Americans continued to practice forms of playing that preserved human dignity.[37] For example, the

---

31. Ibid.
32. Miller, *God and Games.*
33. McFague, *Metaphorical Theology.*
34. Handelman, *Models and Mirrors.*
35. Cox, *Feast of Fools.*
36. Ricoeur, *Essays on Biblical Interpretation,* 99–104; Walton, "Poetics," 173–82.
37. Evans, *Playing,* 21–28.

"corn shucking ritual" allowed slaves to poke fun at the master under the guise of frivolity.[38] Laughing, singing, and joking, teams of slaves—each led by a "general"—would compete to see which team could be the first to remove the husks from a pile of raw corn. After shucking and feasting, "the master was hoisted up into the air and he and the mistress were made fun of by the black folk," which was made acceptable under the pretense of good fun.[39] However, playing allowed African Americans to experience who they truly were and to reject racist understandings of slaves imposed in everyday life. In playing, they engaged in revelatory experiencing.

Escapist approaches to playing assume that playing is a kind of illusion, as understood in the American social imagination, which has been shaped by Freud and popular culture. Freud understands illusion as the fulfillment of a wish that has no regard for its relation to reality.[40] In this sense, illusions come close to delusions, which are contradictions of reality.[41] As a result of Freud's influential body of work, illusions are often taken as evidence of error or mental instability. Unfortunately, popular American culture does not lend helpful connotations to the term *illusion* either. Being under an illusion implies trickery or deception. A magician does something to give the appearance of reality to fool the audience. In essence, the illusion is a lie meant to mask what is real or true. Associating play with illusion forecloses the possibility of revelatory experiencing, which involves life-giving wisdom coming to light.

A second approach to playing and learning argues for the role of playing in fostering human development.[42] Developmental approaches hold more potential for opening up revelatory experiencing. Beginning with Karl Groos at the end of the nineteenth century, playing has been thought to contribute to children's growth and development. Groos makes inferences about human play from the play of young animals, understanding play in terms of evolutionary process. Widely accepted at the time, Groos argues that human instincts are the foundation of children playing.[43] Like all animals of higher intelligence, human beings play in youth as a preparation

---

38. Ibid., 25.
39. Ibid.
40. Freud, *Future of an Illusion*, 40.
41. Ibid., 39.
42. See literature review in Elkonin, "Theories of Play."
43. Groos, *Play of Animals*, 6–7.

for life.[44] Freud represents another major influence on the way children's play has been understood in developmental terms, but from a psychoanalytic perspective. Freud attributes play to the innate, unconscious need for children to reproduce and address traumatic situations.[45] Other theorists understand the importance of childhood playing in self-teaching. Jean Piaget traces through the span of childhood what a child learns through imitation, the use of symbols, and games with rules.[46] Erik Erikson investigates the role of playing in allowing children to master reality by planning and experiencing model situations, while being protected from real-life consequences and norms.[47]

While studies that involve children serve as a foundation for understanding how playing contributes to human development through the human lifespan, theories of adults playing help to reveal overlap with what is learned later in life. Adults playing in the process of everyday life, which includes but is not limited to leisure, results in heightened creativity in the workplace and self-awareness physically, intellectually, spiritually, and socially.[48] Activities such as listening to music, engaging in religious ritual, or practicing yoga engross adults in experiences that can lead to growth or "self actualization,"[49] while other activities such as folk games and modern sports can help to reinforce social identity.[50] Some of these forms of adult playing can also involve experiences of mastery, where a person engages intellectual or physical challenges and feels successful in meeting them well.[51] Like the playing of childhood, mastery in adult playing involves the pleasure of becoming lost in the "flow" of the experience and accomplishing something.[52] Just as a child's mastery in playing aids in the maturation process, mastery in adult playing implies growth as well as enjoyment.

44. Ibid, 75.

45. Freud, *Beyond the Pleasure Principle*, 15.

46. Piaget, *Play, Dreams, and Imitation*.

47. Erikson, *Childhood and Society*.

48. Blanche, "Play and Process," 263; Caughey, "Mind Games," 30–31; Cheska, "Revival, Survival, and Revisal," 41–42; Mainemelis and Ronson, "Fields of Play"; Meyer, *From Workplace to Playspace*.

49. Blanche, "Play and Process," 30–31.

50. Cheska, "Revival, Survival, and Revisal," 153.

51. Blanche, "Play and Process," 264.

52. Ibid., 263.

While they lend some support for my own conclusions about what adults learn in playing, developmental approaches to playing have limitations for understanding revelatory experiencing in light of playing. Developmental approaches tend to be more focused on playing alone and the development of the individual, making them less insightful for examining revelatory experiencing, which are dependent on the participation of others and of Spirit. Furthermore, revelatory experiencing involves both individual and communal formation in Christian faith, not simply individual development.

Finally, a third approach to the outcomes of playing and learning focuses on creativity, which hold even greater promise for exploring revelatory experiencing. One might place Csikszentmihalyi's work on flow in this category since his argument is about how the experience of playfulness fosters creativity. However, he is careful to specify his interest in the experience of playfulness rather than play.[53] Csikszentmihalyi understands creativity in terms of novelty and innovation, which can impact society, but he is less interested in the social dynamic of playing and what it might change.

Theories in this third approach highlight the creativity of playing, in which playing socializes "not simply by imparting behaviors that integrate the players into their cultural systems, but by providing them with innovative alternatives that they may be able to use to change that cultural system."[54] Brian Sutton-Smith's work has been important in developing this way of approaching play and learning. He proposes that playing involves performance, in which actors dramatize "unmastered arousals and reductions" of everyday life in ways that are life giving.[55] In his view, games, for example, allow "incompatibles outside of play [to be] brought into new forms of synthesis."[56] Drawing on the work of Lev Vygotsky, Sutton-Smith argues that playing allows for the construction of new meaning. In the case of children, the freer the conditions for playing, the more likely they are to "increase[e] flights of reversibility, to cultural parody and amusement" that move toward a changing reality.[57] Adult forms of playing, including ritual, sporting events, celebrations, and performances, allow for the

---

53. Csikszentmihalyi, "Concept of Flow," 257–74.

54. Sutton-Smith, "Epilogue," 315.

55. Ibid., 310.

56. Ibid.

57. Ibid., 308.

"recapitulation" of the balance between primary and secondary emotions.[58] Secondary emotions can be experienced and creatively redressed within the "fiction" that playing allows.[59] This view of playing accounts for darker forms of emotion to be associated with playing—not only fun and delight.[60]

Sutton-Smith is influenced partly by Victor Turner, who recognizes play in both "tribal" rituals and in leisure activities of industrial nations.[61] In Turner's view, there is a spectrum of ritual that has *ludic* (playful) dimensions. On one end, "liminal phenomena" (e.g., rites of passage and rituals based on the calendar) do a great deal of the "'work' of the collectivity" in allowing people to enact symbolically what they believe promotes fertility, avoids disaster, transforms, and heals.[62] Paradoxically, rituals that are liminal allow people to "play with the elements of the familiar and defamiliarize them. Novelty emerges from unprecedented combinations of familiar elements."[63] On the opposite end of the continuum that characterizes ritual, leisure activities (what Turner calls "liminoid" phenomena, including fiestas, Halloween masking, art, and sports events) characterize industrial nations. They exhibit a playful element in that the liminoid can immerse people in an "independent domain of creativity activity,"[64] which can give people the opportunity and permission to be critical of or experiment with the status quo, though in mediated form.[65] Sutton-Smith builds on Turner's ideas of the liminoid, arguing that such playing does not simply maintain cultural systems but possibly changes them through experimentation.[66] However, I tend to give rituals such as liturgy, which Turner would call liminal, more credit for bringing about social change.

Approaches to playing and learning with an eye for creative outcomes are more fruitful for exploring revelatory experiencing. Unlike developmental approaches, they account for both individual and communal learning and becoming. They provide compelling theory as to why children and adults, individuals and communities engage in playing, opening the door

---

58. Sutton-Smith, "Recapitulation Redressed," 15, 17.

59. Ibid, 17.

60. Sutton-Smith, 18

61. Turner, *From Ritual to Theatre*, 52.

62. Ibid., 32.

63. Ibid., 27.

64. Ibid., 33.

65. Ibid,, 40.

66. Sutton-Smith, "Order and Disorder," 17–18.

for seeing playing as a lens for understanding religion and other cultural expressions. Furthermore, the focus on creativity is amenable to theological reflection in that creation and re-creation are theological categories. (This is addressed more fully in the next chapter.) Winnicott's work shares the most affinity with developmental approaches and creativity approaches to playing and learning. However, his work also makes its own contributions to considering revelatory experiencing.

CREATIVITY AND PLAYING AS A FORM OF ENGAGEMENT

Unlike "escapist" approaches that understand playing as a withdrawal from or a denial of reality, I argue that playing is a form of engagement with reality. Losing oneself in a world "as if" is permeated with a sense of illusion, but these illusions are vital to human maturation. From the earliest of days, argues Winnicott, a hungry infant "creates" the breast by making it magically appear on demand. This healthy illusion requires the participation of a caregiver who can anticipate the baby's needs and be attentive and responsive to them. When baby cries, mother interprets this as a need for milk and presents the breast for feeding. The mother or caregiver need not be perfect but "good-enough," as Winnicott says. This illusion allows baby to feel powerful in creating what she is seeking. It gives baby the impression that the world is a reliable and responsive place.[67] By holding and nursing the infant, mother gives baby a critical sense of aliveness or "I am myself."[68] In this model, playing is always between at least two human beings, each of whom needs the other. Baby needs mother's responsiveness, just as much as mother needs baby's response to know what is appropriate. An object relations approach is quite different than "escapist" approaches to playing, in which losing oneself in fantasy can be an individual experience as easily as a communal one.

Playing is a form of relating to reality that emerges in infancy and unfolds through a lifetime.[69] Although the mother attends as well as possible to baby's needs, the infant soon experiences moments of disappointment, when mother is nowhere to be found. The "good enough" mother or

67. Winnicott, *Playing and Reality*, 10; Winnicott, *Child and the Outside World*, 90, 157, 183.

68. Winnicott, *Maturational Processes*, 145, 224.

69. Winnicott, *Playing and Reality*, 18.

caregiver helps baby to cope with her temporary absence and to progress toward weaning by providing possible substitutes (e.g., a blanket, a teddy bear) from which baby can choose. These items, or what we refer to as "things," allow baby to create the illusion of her presence by bringing it to life through the creativity of playing. Winnicott calls these items transitional objects. Adults are not so different from infants and children when unexpected realities crash in. When a hurricane destroys a home, a survivor might salvage some token that evokes memories of the former home. The surviving object brings comfort and continuity with the past as the hurricane victim copes with a new future. The patterns of how an infant navigates reality through playing remain with a person through maturity.

Like other approaches to playing and learning, Winnicott locates playing in the most basic of human relationships, which are first experienced within the family. In the teddy bear or blanket, baby creates and finds a mother substitute to possess or push away. It is important that the space for play is unchallenged,[70] meaning adults know that the "rules" of the adult world do not apply. A good enough parent knows to play along with teddy being real. The everyday choices a family makes to play along with a child's play attest to love and belonging as some of what facilitates playing. Other explanations focus on why human beings seek play (e.g., the need for diversion, the need for mastery, or the need for communal evolution), without attending equally well to why what is created in playing is found. The latter sheds light on facilitating revelatory experiencing.

In a loving and supportive environment, a child is free to explore the many possibilities of playing, to make choices between them, and to experience what emerges. The object allows the child to invent a mother that is at his/her disposal—to cuddle, to talk to, to drag around—all validating a sense of "me" or "mine."[71] However, at some point, the child "destroys" the object mother when it is not being played with, when it is effectively outside of the child's imaginative control.[72] The illusion is dispelled when the object is no longer "alive." When a child realizes the blanket is just a blanket (what Winnicott calls "object use"), an opportunity to sense what is "not-me" also arises. The idea of mother that the object represented drops away (temporarily and later for good), but that gives the child fresh perspective

---

70. Ibid., 17.

71. Winnicott, *Child and the Outside World*, 163.

72. Winnicott, *Piggle*, 189–90.

about the human mother that remains.[73] The child senses by comparison the aspects of mother-in-the-flesh that the object mother embodied only in part. One illusion may crumble, but a new one waits to be created because reality is always bigger than any sliver that can be perceived at a given moment. The process of grasping and integrating reality is never ending.

While playing is critical to the process of human maturation, adult playing may involve less mastery and more cultivation of the habit of playing and openness to authentic relating and to what is emerging. The notion of mastery may be helpful in thinking about children's development but less so in the contexts of adults and in reflecting on revelatory experiencing in particular. Mastery implies a hierarchical sequence in which one accomplishes one stage then moves on from one to the next, as if playing primarily involves acquiring skills or knowledge. It is true that over time playing (in a Winnicottian sense) allows one to become increasingly at ease and adept at relating to others and to reality in ways that are out of the ordinary—with greater authenticity and spontaneity than one might experience at a given moment. A person can gain mastery of various skills or knowledge that certain kinds of playing (as "flow") require. However, playing cultivates openness to being decentered/re-centered and the habit of needing to be more of oneself (with oneself and with others).

The participation of others in playing is key to character building and the building up of community. As human beings reach adulthood, there remains the task of allowing one's understanding of reality to evolve, as the messiness, unpredictability, and mystery of reality continue to impinge on one's perceptions of it. In adulthood, a person engages this task by drawing on an expanded repertoire for engaging reality and one another rooted in what was learned in childhood. Adults retain patterns of negotiating reality through "favorite things" as they did when they were younger. Many adults have their own collection of transitional objects (photos, souvenirs, and mementos) that mediate loss, faith, love and other complexities of life. In addition, adults turn to cultural experience as a means of engaging reality.[74] Adults take in a theatrical play, go to the movies, or worship God (as do children). Essentially, culture provides opportunities to create healthy illusions. Winnicott believed that adults form groups based on shared illusory experiences that allow them to negotiate reality.[75] Joined by a cultural con-

73. Winnicott, *Playing and Reality*, 90.

74. Ibid., 138–39.

75. Ibid., 4.

text, adults practice patterns of dealing with reality that have been tested and refined in community, often by generations of like-minded others.

Within the cultural sphere of Christian community, believers share the experience of seeking and finding connections between the reality of God "out there" (in the universe or in Christian history) and God "in here" (in the intimacy of the heart).[76] This is not so different from the child seeking and finding a "mother substitute" for the flesh-and-blood mother and the child's idea of mother. In the many forms of Christian tradition, the faithful craft with one another their own original experiences from symbols, language, and images provided by churches, making these givens feel real and alive.[77] With the stuff of tradition and their own lives, together people creatively construct images of God and themselves. Over a single lifetime, God-images are created, destroyed, and revised as an individual's faith and understanding of God evolve.[78] The same could be said of Christians in history. Compare God images that were prevalent during the time of Martin Luther to those of contemporary feminist and womanist theologians (both scholars and practitioners), who have deconstructed monolithic, patriarchal God-images and proposed alternatives.[79]

A Winnicottian notion of playing provides some cognate terms (e.g., illusion, transitional object, mother substitute) that help to explain why human beings are shaped by revelatory experiencing throughout life. This borrowed language helps to de-mystify revelatory experiencing—or at least the human part. Human beings engage in experiencing that can be symbolized as revelatory because it is basic to human being, becoming, and belonging with others.

As there are limitations to every approach, Winnicott has limitations when it comes to thinking about revelatory experiencing. His approach accounts for what is created within and in between players. Although he implicitly accounts for the bodily contact between mother and baby, the bodily dimensions of playing could be explored more fully, which is why the language of aesthetics is needed. (I explore this in chapter 5.) The bodily experiences of participants are vital to what is felt, perceived, and known both within, between, and among individuals. The presence of Spirit and others are registered in the body, which constitutes a physical boundary

76. Influenced by Borg, *God We Never Knew*, 12.

77. Ulanov, *Finding Space*, 14.

78. For more on God as a transitional object, see Rizzuto, *Birth of the Living God*, 178.

79. See McFague, *Models of God*; Knight, *Feminist Mysticism*.

between what is "of me" and what is "beyond me." Paying attention to the ways that the senses are evoked in playing gives clues to facilitating revelatory experiencing.

A second limitation of Winnicott's theory is his unfinished work in the area of religion and the arts. He wrote tantalizingly about both, but he stopped short of a fuller account of religion and the arts as playing. His gestures indicate recognition of the potential of culture—and human beings being together in organized ways—to provide some of what a child ideally experiences in the family.

HOW CHRISTIANS PLAY

The ambiguity of playing necessitates a great deal of theoretical groundwork to be able to consider the notion of Christians playing. It is not enough to use social scientific language about playing or theological language about revelatory experiencing. A third approach is needed, which is to consider what playing looks like in the context of Christian tradition, expressed in verbal and behavioral symbols that are familiar yet might appear anew in a conversation about playing.

In retrospect, we have some insights into the lesser-known territory to which both symbols (playing and revelatory experiencing) point. We know this kind of experiencing leads deeper into reality, rather than withdrawing or denying it. We know the participation of others is crucial. We know that this way of engaging reality and one another is fundamental to human being and becoming. We know that something of God that was hidden comes into perception. We know that Spirit has a role in making these experiences powerful and life giving. This kind of experiencing (partly described by the languages of playing and revelatory experiencing) might be recognizable to practitioners even if the languages are less than familiar.

Through ritual, liturgy, and the telling of faith narratives, Christians engage in healthy illusions fostered in playing. These illusions allow the faithful to reach toward life's mysteries and what it means to be human in light of the divine. In the season of Advent, churches set out the appropriate props and materials to reenact and animate the dramatic anticipation of Christ's birth. The Bible, the star, biblical characters, and the stable are familiar and beloved elements of a crèche that allow believers to bring the nativity to life. While these symbols have their own religious meanings, they can also be understood as transitional objects. Stirring creativity and imagination, these Advent images inspire the faithful (at any age) to seek a Christ child that they recreate each year. Believers re-center their lives "as if" Jesus were going to be born for the first time. Advent invites Christians to replay the story of Christ's birth and to pretend they are Mary, Joseph, the wise men, or the shepherds in the story. Believers don the surprise and wonder of the characters of Advent and are formed by the practice of it. Although the outcome of the story is known, the faithful open themselves to the surprise that it might bring. They hope to satisfy a longing to see and experience Christ anew—that Jesus will be born afresh in their hearts.

Acting or believing "as if" is vital for nurturing faith. As David Miller argues, Christian tradition often asks the faithful to act "as if" or consider something "as if" in order to perceive what is spiritually real. In the world of science, a parallel might be conceptualizing an ordinary object, for example, *as if* it were a world of spinning molecules. "[I]n order to be truly at home in the external world, in order to understand what we like to call 'reality,' we have to live poetically. Or as Martin Buber put it: we have to 'imagine the real.' "[80] Likewise in Christian tradition, the faithful are invited to address God as "Our Father, who art in heaven," "as if" "dressed up as Christ."[81] Bread and wine look "as if" they are common elements from a daily meal, but creativity and imagination informed by faith allow them to be experienced as mysteries. The notion of the God's new creation cannot be grasped in any terms other than "as if" because it is both present and not-yet. Being able to re-imagine the world is an eschatological capacity that fosters hope and clarity about what humanity needs to do to usher in the not-yet. Playing helps the faithful deepen the capacity for living in the creative in-between.

Many Christians, including evangelicals in the United States, have rich devotional lives of acting and believing "as if" God were an invisible companion. A study of the Chicago Vineyard found that the faithful were encouraged to pretend "as if" God were sitting right next to them, to talk to God "as if" God were a friend with whom one could spend time, share, or even banter.[82] Though not named as such by practitioners, playing "pretend" is part of evangelical faith that makes God feel more real. The achievement of playing pretend "is to enable someone to treat God as a person, not a packet of rules and propositions, and to draw inferences

80. Miller, *God and Games*, 145.

81. Lewis, *Mere Christianity*, 148–50.

82. Luhrmann, *When God Talks Back*, 74.

about what God thinks and wants that are directly relevant to that person's life."[83] According to the study, pouring God a cup of coffee and sitting down at the table are gestures that suspend disbelief and enact a choice to develop a personal relationship with God.

When Christians are playing together, they are playing at/in God's new creation—where the faithful lose themselves in exploring a world of possibilities in Christ so that they might live into them more fully. In playing *at* the new creation, Christian communities attempt to create the world to which Jesus' life, death, and resurrection point—a place where all of creation can live in justice, harmony, and authenticity. In this play world lit by the Gospel, Christians are called to engage in the creative act of seeing one another truly as brothers and sisters in Christ. In the Eucharist (a structure for playing), the faithful sense the reality to which Christians are called by believing "as if" and being reconciled to one another and to God in the sharing of Christ's body. Oneness as God's children is not a fact to memorize or to mark off on a mental checklist (as in "Got that!"), but a mystery to be contemplated in the heart-spirit and performed by body-mind. Over time Christians are formed by repeated experiences of playing together at/in the new creation.

Paradoxically, Christian communities are sometimes playing *in* God's new creation, which has both a "not-yet" and "already" dimension. At times, the Bible refers to the kingdom of God, which resonates with the notion of the new creation. One of the Pharisees asks Jesus when the kingdom of God is coming, and he replies, "The kingdom of God is not coming with things that can be observed; nor will they say, 'Look, here it is!' or 'There it is!' For, in fact, the kingdom of God is among you."[84] A helpful way of imagining how the kingdom could be "among" the faithful already is to fathom that the kingdom of God is also "within."[85] In other words, it is within the capacity of human beings to constitute the kingdom of God by virtue of something innate that God has granted—being children of God. This "not-yet" and "already" dimension of revelatory experiences are theological ways of referring to what acting or believing "as if" is also attempting to describe in the language of playing. Many Christians find meaning in the metaphor "kingdom of God." However, I refer to God's new creation in this book because it helps to avoid patriarchal language and it

83. Ibid., 92.
84. Luke 17:20–21.
85. Dykstra, "Unrepressing," 394–95.

may be a more open-ended metaphor that people of diverse faiths might find more accessible.

Playing together is one of the multiple ways that Christians may become acquainted with themselves and others as children of God. Children have a marvelous capacity to express more easily than adults authentic thoughts and feelings, to be creative, and to be spontaneous. Growing up tends to result in leaving behind some of those gifts. However, Jesus admonishes his disciples to become like children in order to enter the kingdom of God.[86] Playing invites the faithful to live into being children of God, helping adults to realize their capacity to love and trust one another and God, to respond spontaneously to Spirit, and to create together for the sake of God's new creation. Coming into greater awareness of being children of God encourages Christians to move in the world with confidence, purpose, and a sense of freedom and creativity—how human beings are meant to live. Indirectly, they come to know *true self*, a term borrowed from Winnicott. Here my theology comes closer to Jaco Hamman's understanding of being "play-full," which fosters the kind of peace and justice that God intends.[87] My own understanding has greater emphasis on the "as if" quality of playing.

Winnicott's insight is that a human being behaves in ways that range from spontaneous creativity to guarded, routinized, or scripted behavior. As long as a person feels free and safe enough, she can express some measure of spontaneity or creativity. Winnicott describes this way of being as the "true self," which he believes is central and instinctual to being human.[88] A person does not feel alive or real if true self languishes, yet paradoxically true self cannot be fully known because it must be hidden. Everyday life is too vulnerable a place. For dealing with day-to-day interactions, human beings adopt ways of being in the world that provide some protection. Sometimes it feels necessary to conform to routines or to social norms that one believes will avoid the disapproval of others. Healthy individuals do this some of the time. Less healthy people consistently and unconsciously perform a self that conforms to what they believe will be acceptable to others, with no room for creativity or spontaneity. Winnicott associates these ways of being with what he calls the "false self."[89] A person is always negotiating

---

86. Matthew 18:3.

87. Hamman, *Play-full Life*, 7.

88. Winnicott, *Maturational Processes*, 140.

89. Ibid., 142–43.

between true self and false self according to what feels safe and appropriate at a given moment. If one feels the constant need for false self, it can lead to feeling dead, not real, or inauthentic, but false self cannot be banished. Likewise, one cannot consciously "liberate" true self, as if it were an identity to be made public. Because it is hidden, true self can and must be known indirectly. For Winnicott, culture provides opportunities for true self to "communicate" through intermediate experience.[90] For Christians, this is how the faithful come to know themselves as children of God.

Religion and other forms of cultural experience provide a space in which the faithful are invited to experience true self in response to the presence of others and the Spirit of God. In the drama of acting and believing "as if," the faithful are coaxed by Spirit to venture forth, to forget themselves, and to engage in irresistible play with sacred objects, images, music, texts and memory. The structures of playing offer enough cover to respect the vulnerability of experiencing spontaneity and authenticity, providing mediated forms through which these can be known. When playing has ended, believers gain perspective on the very things that make protective layers feel necessary—what is "not me."

Some religious educators and philosophers who have adopted the notion of true self/false self have also recognized a role for religious education in fostering true self.[91] Thomas Merton, a Trappist monk who was influenced by Buddhist philosophy, believed that true self is rooted in God but is hindered by the false (or external) self, which is dominated by egocentric desires. In Merton's thinking, the purpose of Christian formation is to clear away the illusory false self so that one can sink into true self as God intends.[92] His understanding of false self is in contrast to Winnicott's, who views false self as essential to the human psyche, rather than something to eliminate. Although Winnicott and Merton use the same terms *true self* and *false self*, in doing so Merton is not discussing play.

Berryman cites Winnicott's understanding and language of true self in arguing for "Godly play," which is "the playing of a game that can awaken us to new ways of seeing ourselves as human beings."[93] He recognizes that when children or adults are playing, they experience the surprise of catching a "glimpse of the true self," as they inhabit the space between the "me"

90. Winnicott, *Maturational Processes*, 187–88.

91. Merton, *New Seeds*, 7.

92. Ibid., 34.

93. Berryman, *Godly Play*, 7.

and the "not me."[94] He says, "Godly play is growth-enhancing, because it is a place where one can be not only with the true self but also the true self of others."[95] In Berryman's work, there seems to be no account of false self, despite his use of Winnicott. He argues that Godly play is not only for children but also for adults; however, in his view, adults play by facilitating children's play.[96]

Berryman's understanding of Godly play differs from my understanding of playing in that he frames play exclusively in terms of games, including the "Religion Game" and the "Godly Game." He argues that certain activities (e.g., a computer's simulation of traffic flow) are not games because the outcomes do not involve winning or losing.[97] Berryman identifies salvation as what one "wins" from the "Religion Game," but it is not clear what losing looks like. He writes that games cannot be too easily won, or impossible to win, or guaranteed to win.[98] While I recognize that some playing involves games, not all playing does. Furthermore, the notion of games is less helpful for understanding revelatory experiencing. Following his logic, Berryman's theology implies that in Christianity, salvation is difficult to attain and uncertain. The role that grace plays in the theological economy of the "Religion Game" is unclear.

Like Berryman, Parker Palmer, an educational philosopher informed by the Quaker tradition, also addresses true self, but Palmer is more like Winnicott in believing that true self must be known indirectly. He understands true self as soul, a God-given divine spark that is mysterious, shy, and wise.[99] Although he does not use the language of play, Palmer identifies childhood as a time when human beings are closest to true self as they immerse themselves in fantasy stories and pretend places. Essentially, he describes playing. Palmer argues that when children become adolescents, they often feel the pressure to conform to social roles of the grown up world.[100] Adults who are estranged from their true self experience an "empty self." Like Winnicott, Palmer says that people who feel empty have a sense of

---

94. Ibid., 11.
95. Ibid., 7.
96. Ibid., 24–41.
97. Ibid., 3
98. Ibid., 7.
99. Palmer, *Hidden Wholeness*, 33, 92.
100. Ibid., 15.

something missing in their lives. They feel fraudulent or inauthentic.[101] Winnicott differs from Palmer in discussing how the infant moves between true and false self as he/she relates with mother. While the psychoanalyst recognizes that people negotiate true and false self their entire lives, Palmer implies that humans tend to mature out of true self and tend toward an "empty self." However, Palmer helpfully advocates for the role of spiritual communities ("circles of trust") in helping true self to be known indirectly, which resonates with a Winnicottian view of playing.[102]

The language of playing from Winnicott is helpful and necessary to explore what is lived in revelatory experiencing. However, more theological concepts and ideas are needed to explore further what psychoanalytic (and psychological) concepts and ideas do not reveal. The next step is to engage in theological reflection about revelatory experiencing by thinking more critically about playing, Spirit, and God's new creation.

101. Ibid., 16.
102. Ibid., 52–69.

chapter 3

PLAYING THEOLOGICALLY: LEANING INTO GOD'S NEW CREATION

Each theological perspective on playing varies in its helpfulness in shedding light on what is lived in revelatory experiencing because each one has a different aim. One classic approach is "play theology," which attempts to apply what is known about playing "to ailing or otherwise obtuse and abstract theology, thereby giving it new life."[1] A second traditional approach is "theology of play," in which "one presumably confronts an unknown but happy mystery, the phenomenon of play, with something well-known in advance, a viable form of classical theology."[2] Both play theology and theology of play attempt to provide sound arguments for playing in an effort to overcome ambivalence toward play in some Christian traditions. Both play theology and theology of play tend to reflect systematic theological commitments, whose goal is to deepen theological understanding for its own sake, rather than improve practice.

A drawback of play theology and theology of play is that they do not treat playing as something one does. This creates a strange disconnect from life experience. They refer to playing as a metaphor (e.g., religion is a game), borrowing implicitly from common understandings of play. Any discussion of playing is bound to use play as a metaphor to some degree. However, something vital is missing from a conversation that does not specify what playing looks like, how it relates to particular contexts, or how one might improve the practice of playing and enrich theological reflection. Depending on their lack of sensitivity toward experience, play theology

1. Miller, *God and Games*, xvii.
2. Ibid.

and theology of play tend to be limited in providing insight about what is lived in revelatory experiencing.

While play theology and theology of play characterized theological reflection in the 1970s, more recent work reflects more practical theological commitments. Playing is something not only to think about philosophically and theologically, but also a practice to experience and cultivate with greater intention, drawing on both theological and other interdisciplinary conversation partners. Practical theological approaches to playing vary in how they engage theology and/or other theories. However, they do now advocate for the value of playing with greater awareness of the difference that playing makes for Christian faith and/or ministry. Playing is understood, variously, as a practice for rest and renewal,[3] for discernment and individual encounters with Spirit,[4] and for improving ministry[5] and children's ministry in particular.[6] This practical theological work does not fall neatly into the "escapist" approaches to playing and learning, developmental approaches, or creative approaches outlined in the last chapter. Practical theological approaches may constitute their own category, where playing is understood as strategy for strengthening Christian life, formation, and ministry.

In this chapter, I offer a theological approach to playing that will contribute to theorizing revelatory experiencing and eventually to offering constructive proposals. To begin, I analyze Jürgen Moltmann's *Theology of Play*. Compared to his other works, Moltmann's writing on play is less well known, but it is significant. While *Theology of Play* has its weaknesses, it can be retrieved in light of the larger corpus of his scholarship, including his reflections on the Holy Spirit, love, and the kingdom of God. After introducing his original text, I critique and revise Moltmann's work with an eye toward revelatory experiencing. I then use key ideas in Moltmann as a fresh approach to biblical texts that address the role of Spirit in playing.

3. Johnston, *Christian at Play*; Hamman, *Play-full Life*.

4. Jones, *Holy Play*.

5. Jones, *Jazz of Preaching*; Koppel, *Open-Hearted Ministry*.

6. Elkin, "Role of Play"; Berryman, *Godly Play*; Miller-McLemore, "Royal Road," 505–19.

MOLTMANN MISUNDERSTOOD

Moltmann's *Theology of Play* was roundly criticized in its time. Three contemporaries—Robert Neale, Sam Keen, and David Miller—wrote responses that were published in the volume. Pained by their criticisms, Moltmann writes, "[T]he premises from which these replies have been written are not the same as my own—not in the least. . . . I am at a loss as to what to answer to these three American [theological] approaches to play. The authors and I live in the same one world, and yet in completely different inner spaces."[7] Moltmann was baffled that he was "not playing in the same ballpark" as his colleagues.[8] In general, their criticism reflects certain assumptions and commitments that shape the readers' respective interpretations of the text. While no work is without flaws, Moltmann's critics held certain expectations of what a theology of play should look like and misunderstood the work because it did not match their expectations. One can see how easily this could happen given the multiple meanings of play and the many theological approaches to playing.

From the title of the book, one might expect (as did his critics) that Moltmann's primary goal was to use theological concepts to understand the phenomenon of playing, but instead he wrote a play theology. At the time that he wrote his book, Moltmann was concerned about distinguishing Christian faith from social activism, lest faith be reduced to justifying political aims.[9] In his preface, he writes that his goal is "to reassert the value of aesthetic joy against the absolute claims of ethics."[10] His critique of ethics is that without aesthetics, ethics can devolve into legalism and an over-focus on achievement, and that ethics alone can place undue attention on guarding against what is deemed to be "bad" behavior.[11] (Conversely, aesthetics must also be informed by ethics or else they become "empty."[12]) Linking play with beauty, celebration, and expression, play is an aesthetic "world symbol" for Moltmann. He writes, "Play as world symbol goes beyond the categories of doing, having, and achieving and leads us into the categories

---

7. Moltmann, *Theology of Play*, 111.

8. Ibid.

9. McDougall, *Pilgrimage of Love*, 18.

10. Moltmann, *Theology of Play*, vii.

11. Ibid., 23, 43.

12. Ibid., 43.

of being, of authentic human existence and demonstrative rejoicing in it."[13] Moltmann uses the symbol of play to illumine the experience of living in Christ. He assumes that by first experiencing the joy of celebrating the resurrection, one can then begin to embrace the possibilities of God's new creation and embody it in acts of love.[14]

In *Theology of Play*, Moltmann does not use the language of experience, but this is essentially what he discusses. (He later uses the language of experience to discuss "experiences of the Spirit."[15]) For example, rather than focusing solely on "church-for-the-world" or "church-for-others" with the emphasis on specific action to address the needs of the world, he advocates for "being-there-for-others" and "being-with-others," which shifts the emphasis to relationship. Moltmann is concerned with the *experience* of both the oppressed and people of good will who wish to help. He fears that merely acting on behalf of others (e.g., charity) can unwittingly promote paternalism even if well-intended actions provide assistance. Rather, by also being with each other in life-giving ways (i.e., by playing), Christians constitute the "congregation of the liberated," embodying liberation in its very being.[16] In other words, the playing of the faithful is a way of being with/for others that is liberating. Later in the book, I will use Moltmann's notion of being with/for others to understand why cases of revelatory experiencing are transformative.

Moltmann's understanding of play as "being-there-with/for-others" resonates with Winnicott's notion of playing as relational engagement, in which mother and child are not only *with* but *there for* one another. Moltmann refers to being with and for the oppressed, which means being in joyous solidarity with those who are suffering. His interest in mutuality and empowerment as opposed to charity is striking. Like Winnicott, he is deeply concerned about being with others in life-giving ways. Both these towering figures published on play in the same year but in different fields, and both use the language of playing to describe the experience of human connection and becoming—Winnicott from a psychoanalytic perspective, Moltmann from a theological one.

Even in writing, Moltmann is aware of thinking about play in ways that his contemporaries in theology do not. Anticipating the possibility of

---

13. Ibid., 23.

14. McDougall, *Pilgrimage of Love*, 18.

15. Moltmann, *Spirit of Life*, 17–77.

16. Moltmann, *Theology of Play*, 71.

being misunderstood, he acknowledges that his approach to playing and "games of liberation" is "foreign to an understanding of the game as self-forgetting pleasure."[17] Moltmann is wary of "escapist" understandings of play, which he realizes are prevalent. To alert readers to his unconventional rhetorical strategy, he notes, "We shall attempt to move from a critical analysis of games in terms of their outward appearance in society to a critical analysis of society in terms of an inside view of games."[18] Discussing the outward appearance of games focuses on what is happening—much like a commentator reports what is happening on the field play-by-play. Instead, Moltmann tries to address an "inside view" of playing or what players are experiencing. He describes the experience of playing in aesthetic and affective terms—as joyous, beautiful, freeing, and hopeful. His account of playing seems idyllic (it is, and therefore problematic without revision), but he intends his notion of playing to have an edge. He argues, "Play should liberate, not tranquilize, awaken, and not anesthetize. Liberating play is protest against the evil plays of the oppressor and the exploiter. Thus play seriously and fight joyously!"[19] Looking back nearly thirty years later, he admits that he had in mind a "revolutionary Christianity" that would "turn the wretched condition of the world into what was good, just, and living by virtue of its hope."[20] Moltmann is referring to the early part of his writing career, when *Theology of Hope* was published in 1964. However, *Theology of Play* (1971) was written roughly in the same period.

Moltmann's theology of play is inseparable from his political theology, which calls for justice and social transformation, and these two streams are to be understood as intertwined.[21] In his thinking, "[t]he believer, who first experiences the joy of faith and a foretaste of the coming kingdom [captured in the symbol of playing], begins to experiment with the kingdom's liberating possibilities and to put them into praxis."[22] He writes about the joy and delight of playing as part of his doxological theology, which he continues to develop alongside his political theology.[23] Most interpreters of Moltmann's work shy away from his appeals to believers' affections and

---

17. Ibid., 6.

18. Ibid.

19. Ibid., 113.

20. Moltmann, "Hope and Reality," 78.

21. McDougall, *Pilgrimage of Love*, 18.

22. Ibid.

23. Ibid., 16–22.

imagination,[24] which helps to explain why *Theology of Play* has often been discounted or neglected. The author himself is aware of his doxological theology being perceived as less than rigorous.[25]

Moltmann is a systematic theologian who increasingly did the work of practical theology throughout his career, though he did not call it such.[26] In *Theology of Play*, he writes, "*Christian theology* is . . . the *theory of a practice* which alleviates human need."[27] He emphasizes theologizing as an act of imagination, which he assumes has the power to enact change by envisioning the new. Taking stock in the power of visioning, Moltmann thinks of theology as "pure theory" or "a point of view which transforms the viewer into that which he views."[28] He implies that theologizing is a transformative practice. Reflecting on his career in 2000, Moltmann writes, "From the theology of liberation that was now beginning [in the 1960s] we learnt a theology closer to praxis than we were academically used to."[29] He declares his commitment to praxis in *The Trinity and the Kingdom* (1991), mirroring liberation theology's focus on praxis for the sake of liberating the oppressed.[30] His theological method has been described as "critical praxis correlation," in which theology and practices are in dialectical relationship with one another.[31]

Yet Moltmann's notion of playing is underdeveloped, especially from a practical theological perspective. He does not discuss extensively playing either as a concept or as a practice, though he does convey his sense of the experience of playing. Playing games is a combination of "sincerity and mirth, suspension and relaxation," in which a player is fully absorbed and takes seriously.[32] The player transcends him/herself as well as the game, gaining freedom without losing it.[33] Enjoyment is key in Moltmann's understanding of playing because "[t]he glorification of God lies in the de-

24. Ibid., 22.

25. Moltmann, *Experiences in Theology*, xvi. Cited in McDougall, *Pilgrimage of Love*, 22.

26. Meeks, "Moltmann's Contribution," 57–74.

27. Moltmann, *Theology of Play*, 27.

28. Ibid.

29. Moltmann, *Experiences in Theology*, 217.

30. McDougall, *Pilgrimage of Love*, 20.

31. Chopp, *Praxis of Suffering*, 139–42. Cited in McDougall, *Pilgrimage of Love*, 21.

32. McDougall, *Pilgrimage of Love*, 18.

33. Ibid.

monstrative joy of existence."[34] Unfortunately, he neither gives a context for playing nor suggests what might further playing. Playing is less of a practice than an experience of spontaneity. He deliberately does not give examples or prescriptions, which he feels unwittingly inhibit spontaneity.[35] Spontaneity "*cannot* be done, only released or set free."[36] Moltmann does not write as an educator who considers how such experiences might be facilitated.

Moltmann's recognition of spontaneity in the nature of playing gives him an interesting connection with Winnicott. Identifying spontaneity as key to playing, both theorists recognize that playing invites authenticity. Moltmann recognizes spontaneity as evidence of being able to live into greater spiritual authenticity as children of God, who are born to be joyous and free. Winnicott sees the spontaneity of playing as a sign of true self being able to relate to others in authentic, creative ways. Winnicott is more open-ended than Moltmann by not specifying what authenticity looks like for a person. The theologian and the psychoanalyst do not understand spontaneity in exactly the same way, though they are not unrelated. For Moltmann, spontaneity is unfettered, unabashed reveling or playfulness that one experiences when engaged in a game. For Winnicott, spontaneity may include experiencing playfulness, but it primarily involves being freely creative in ways that are revealing of oneself, which might include daring to express oneself or participating in what is risky, momentous, and not fully known. Although Winnicott gives a fuller account of the spontaneity of playing, both theologian and psychoanalyst recognize the formative role of playing for spiritual and psychic maturity.

I find it plausible that Moltmann turned to play as a symbol for preliminary ideas that he developed more fully using other language. He was probably attracted to the notion of play because he recognized the power of imagination, affect, and freedom. He later writes, "Theology ought not to be just 'the doctrine of faith' . . . [I]t ought to be creative imagination for God's coming kingdom."[37]

Having introduced Moltmann's *Theology of Play*, I turn to highlighting useful ideas of his, deconstructing the work, and reconstructing it with an eye for deepening a theory of revelatory experiencing.

---

34. Ibid., 21.

35. Ibid., 70.

36. Ibid.

37. Moltmann, "Hope and Reality," 78; ibid., *Coming of God*, xiv.

ASSESSING AND DECONSTRUCTING MOLTMANN'S THEOLOGY OF PLAY

In *Theology of Play*, Moltmann argues that Easter signals the "new game of freedom" revealed in Jesus Christ. He uses the metaphor of games to signal a paradigm shift between one way of thinking, feeling, and doing to another—from "dominion through games" to "games of liberation," from old to new.[38] Easter is the ultimate joke that reverses the fear and guilt-mongering of "powers and rulers of this world," which keep humanity enslaved.[39] Moltmann describes the new life established in Christ in terms of playing—a life of freedom, rejoicing, and abundance for all. The "new game" heralds and sweeps up people in a new creation that will echo the first creation, made out of God's free will and pleasure.[40] In raising Christ, argues Moltmann, God's intent was not simply to wash away sin and "restore the ancient play of creation," but to have a new relationship with humanity in which God guides people to the new future that God is bringing about.[41] In my view, Moltmann's description of the resurrection as God's play reinforces the relational nature of revelation, in which God and humanity are in life-giving relationship with one another.

Moltmann's understanding of playing as a transformative process positions him well to contribute to a discussion of revelatory experiencing. The significance of playing "games of liberation" is that they "construct 'anti-environments' and 'counter-environments' (McLuhan) to ordinary and everyday human environments."[42] Although constructing counter-environments can give rise to lies, distorted illusions, or unhealthy fantasies, such actions can also be transformative or liberative.[43] For example, political satire exposes the oppressed to some truths about their situation and contributes to their liberation.[44] Rather than escaping reality, helping people to cope, or allowing people to remain the same, games of liberation confront and open people up to "creative freedom and future alternatives.

---

38. Moltmann, *Theology of Play*, 3.

39. Ibid., 30.

40. Ibid., 17, 26.

41. Ibid., 26.

42. McLuhan, *Understanding Media*. Cited in Moltmann, *Theology of Play*, 12.

43. Steiner, *After Babel*.

44. Moltmann, *Theology of Play*, 13.

... [W]e are increasingly playing with the future in order to get to know it."[45] Moltmann illumines the pedagogical implications of playing: a "conscious confrontation" of what a play world challenges learners to know.[46] For him, an anti-environment is not so much a social and linguistic construct as one that allows learners to speak and imagine differently.[47] Moltmann's claim attests to the value of playing as an *experience* of a counter-environment, where learners feel, see, and know newness from the living of it. Here my own thinking about revelatory experiencing as decentering/re-centering resonates with Moltmann's understanding of the value of playing. For him and for me, this liberative playing that immerses and confronts people is not at all disconnected from revelation. In fact, it is necessary for moving toward the new creation to which Christ's resurrection points.

Moltmann provides me with insight about the spectrum upon which revelation and revelatory experiencing exist, including how the two are related. In every generation the significance of Christian revelation and divine revelation continues (in part) to unfold and transform through revelatory experiencing. In these everyday experiences of living in light of Easter, Christians come to know what is vital. For Moltmann, Easter life is "preplay" that gives the faithful a "prevision of the future life of rejoicing."[48] There is something odd in calling the playing of the faithful "preplay," as if present practice were not truly playing. However, Moltmann's emphasis is on the anticipatory nature of playing, which helps the faithful to grasp what is present and what is to come and therefore to have hope. Throughout his career, he continues to write about Easter as a "history-making event" whose significance lies in its unfinished character.[49] Moltmann's notion of playing gives me language to discuss how Christians live in light of the resurrection, anticipating the new creation, and living in the present.

Moltmann's ideas support the notion of playing as a formative, aesthetic experience for Christian faith, as I argue in chapter 5. The language of playing allows Moltmann to call attention to what Christians already know in the experience of playing, drawing from "the world of primal childhood trust."[50] He understands that the felt sense of spontaneity and freedom in

45. Ibid., 12–13

46. Ibid., 12.

47. Steiner, *After Babel*, 57–58; Hart, "Imagination," 58.

48. Moltmann, *Theology of Play*, 35.

49. Moltmann, *Theology of Hope*, 139, 180–81; Moltmann, *Crucified God*, 105–6.

50. Moltmann, *Theology of Play*, 35.

playing is important for grasping what God's new creation (a symbol) is like, thereby transforming the faithful's habits of being with others. He says, "We are playing in the world and with the world, and we are trying through free play to make ourselves fit for the totally-other."[51] Moltmann understands that the experience of playing helps people to know what they could not know otherwise, which he tries to capture in his reference to "counter-environments," though this concept needs to be further developed.

I also find it helpful that Moltmann identifies the church as a key place for the kind of liberative playing he describes. He calls the church to be a "testing ground" of the kingdom of God. He hopes that churches will become models of creative freedom, a place where "productive imagination" is fostered so that people can envision the future and awaken their spontaneity.[52] He briefly mentions "liberated churches" that he has seen in the United States, Kenya, and Germany, though he gives details neither on what playing looks like in these contexts nor on how these churches came to play more fully than others.[53] Nevertheless, he identifies churches as vital places where playing is taking place and where he hopes Christians will experience faith more often. Moltmann encourages me to take seriously the role of churches in facilitating playing.

Unfortunately, Moltmann is too narrow in specifying the experiences of playing as only joyous or delightful. He links human playing with the play of the creator, believing both are expressions of free will and pleasure. Associating play mainly with joy and pleasure is understandable given his search for a strong antidote to what robs people of hope, but an understanding of playing that lacks texture does not ring true of the kingdom. While there is surely joy and pleasure in God's new creation, in my view experiences of authenticity and of becoming more and more oneself ("being true self," in Winnicott's words) are what is truly liberating. Seeing and accepting people as they are constitute practices that embody God's new creation, even when honesty, compassion, and vulnerability are hard. Unfortunately, that Moltmann romanticizes the nature of playing leads him to make some troubling contrasts.

Moltmann dichotomizes play and work, pleasure and struggle, aesthetics and ethics. In his view, Christians do not come to life-saving knowledge of God's new creation via ethics alone, through struggle for

51. Ibid., 16.

52. Ibid., 70.

53. Ibid.

achievement, through work, or through the enforcement of laws. They come to know God's new creation through "moments of grace and faith, of joy and love, of openness and hope, and not in the moments of glory due to achievement and efforts."[54] His view reifies playing, elevating it to what is hopeful, joyous, or delightful, while depicting work in caricature, reducing it to what is arduous and slavish. Both characterizations do not do justice to the complexity of playing or working for justice, which can evoke many emotions that do not easily fall into these dichotomies. Furthermore, it is not clear why one should associate playing exclusively with aesthetics or struggle and achievement with ethics. Such binary thinking about playing versus working makes it more difficult to imagine how ethics and aesthetics are integrally related, which Moltmann wishes to argue. His overly romantic view of playing, which is at the heart of these problematic contrasts, will be reframed below in light of his larger work.

MOLTMANN REVISED: SPIRIT AND PLAYING FOR LOVE'S SAKE

Although Moltmann does not address Spirit in his theology of play, one can analyze his work on play in light of his reflections on the Holy Spirit, and in this way illuminate his theology of play.[55] Had his work on playing been better understood and appreciated by his peers, he might have written more on play as he continued to develop his ideas about Spirit and the kingdom of God. For Moltmann, Spirit is the link between God's creation of the world, the person and the life of Jesus Christ, and God's continual being in the world.[56] His thinking about Spirit enriches his earlier thinking about play in relation to all three of these. In what follows, I address Moltmann's *Theology of Play* and his larger work on Spirit in relation to three events of Christian history—creation, the resurrection, and kingdom of God. In each case, I make inferences from Moltmann's corpus to help extend his original work on play (what I will refer to as "Moltmann revised"), while at the same time addressing weaknesses of his treatise on play.

First, in *Theology of Play* Moltmann addresses the creation of the world as God's play, and elsewhere he argues that God has created life through

---

54. Moltmann, *Theology of Play*, 35.

55. For a literature review, see Guttesen, *Leaning*.

56. Ibid., 82–83; Moltmman, *Spirit of Life*, 60–71.

Spirit.[57] In creating life, God plays out of God's "good will or pleasure," not necessity.[58] Moltmann writes, "Hence the creation is God's play, a play of [God's] groundless and inscrutable wisdom. It is the realm in which God displays [God's] glory."[59] Though he does not give an example, I imagine that the theologian has the glories of nature in mind when he associates God's good will or pleasure with the play of creation. What is notable is that the play of creation *displays*. It reveals mystery and truth about God if only in part. However, Moltmann's other writing suggests a refinement of his thinking about creation, as he reflects on the creative, revelatory role of Spirit. He argues that through Spirit, God created human beings and all creatures to be in relationship to God, keeping them open to this future in Spirit.[60] God's creation of life through Spirit is part of the long preparation for what is to come. Analyzing his two approaches to creation, I infer from Moltman's thinking that God plays through Spirit, making perceptible in creation part of what God has promised.

Moltmann's reflections on creation and God's *kenosis* as an outpouring of God's love help to soften some of his early, strong associations of God's play with pleasure and delight. In reflecting on play he argues that God "has brought forth [God's] creation to enjoy it, to display its splendor and in all things that glorify himself."[61] Elsewhere he writes of God's "necessary resolve" to create out of the unity of God in three persons and their perfect love.[62] Although Moltmann does not explicitly associate play with love in his *Theology of Play*, I would construct a revision of his work based on linking play and love. In Moltmann revised, God as creator plays not simply out of free will and pleasure but also out of love, so that the play of creation has its being in God and God dwells in creation, much like the persons of the Trinity dwell in one another.[63] Love is a key theme for much of Moltmann's work. He argues that God limits Godself in creating the world, so that God's beloved creatures have freedom to become.[64] From my perspective, love

---

57. Moltmann, *Way of Jesus Christ*, 91–94, 288–90; Moltmann, *History and the Triune God*, 133–34.

58. Moltmann, *Theology of Play*, 17.

59. Ibid.

60. Moltmann, *History and the Triune God*, 129, 133.

61. Moltmann, *Theology of Play*, 18.

62. Moltmann, *God in Creation*; Moltmann, *Spirit of Life*, 71–73.

63. Moltmann, *History and the Triune God*, 127.

64. Moltmann, "God's Kenosis," 147.

provides a broader, more robust frame for understanding God's purpose for creating the world. Love can still account for God's playful pleasure and free will in creating, but as I argue below, love is a fuller, more convincing explanation for the relationship between play and the resurrection, as well as play and God's new creation.

The second major event of Christian history that Moltmann reflects on is Christ's resurrection. He addresses the resurrection in terms of play in his treatise, but elsewhere he speaks more often about the resurrection in terms of Spirit. Granted, in *Theology of Play* he avoids calling the resurrection an act of divine playing, but it is implied in his image of Easter as making a laughing stock of death.[65] He also implies God's play in the resurrection as he takes Harvey Cox to task for not taking the resurrection more seriously in Cox's image of "Christ as Harlequin."[66] Elsewhere Moltmann expresses a strong pneumatological understanding of Jesus' life, his resurrection, and the kingdom of God, which I think can reframe his thinking on play and Easter. He argues that the Holy Spirit through which God created the world is also in Jesus.[67] In the life of Jesus, Spirit makes visible the kingdom of God.[68] Not only is Jesus raised by the power of Spirit, he ascends and sends the Spirit so that he might be present in the world.[69]

In Moltmann revised, one gathers a fuller picture as one reflects on his understanding of play and the resurrection in light of his work on Spirit. One can infer that the mystery and creativity of Spirit are at the heart of the resurrection, when God plays the ultimate joke on death in the most unexpected event in history. The revelatory nature of God's play in creation shows itself at the resurrection, with Spirit as the creative love behind both events. In light of his understanding of love, God's play in the resurrection is a loving, gracious surprise that transforms everything. In a reconstructed version of Moltmann, understanding love as the basis for divine playing makes sense in light of the resurrection. One can imagine that God raised Jesus out of God's good pleasure and free will, and perhaps even more compellingly, one can believe that God brings him back from the dead out of love for the Son and for all of God's creation. Both explanations ring true.

65. Moltmann, *Theology of Play*, 30.

66. Ibid., 29.

67. Moltmann, *Way of Jesus Christ*, 91–94

68. Ibid., 73.

69. Moltmann, *History and the Triune God*, 84.

God plays "for love's sake" [70]—both in creating the world and in resurrecting Christ.

Moltmann's most passionate argument is for Easter life as playing, but here again his larger work on Spirit and love help to nuance his writing on play. In *Theology of Play*, he suggests that the only appropriate response to the resurrection is for human beings to play, rejoicing in and celebrating God's wondrous surprise that overturns death. Just as Easter captures the hope of Christ, playing allows Christians to embody hope as all of creation continues to struggle toward the kingdom. Moltmann's rationale is that because God's play emanates from God's good will and pleasure, human beings glorify God in their playing and consequently their enjoyment of life. However, this creates a moral bind for Moltmann. He struggles with the question of how some people are free to play while others are not. He asks, "How can we laugh and rejoice when there are still so many tears to be wiped away when new tears are being added every day?" [71] Moltmann's solution is that the joy of playing is the antidote to despair, mimicking God's laugher in the face of death. However, his thinking about play in light of his work on love provides a stronger response.

In Moltmann revised, if human beings play for love's sake (as God does), then the goal of playing is not simply free enjoyment of life that defies oppression as Moltmann envisions. Instead, playing involves experiencing authenticity in our creative, loving search for being-with/for-one-another. Being able to be authentic in playing, we come to know one another in Christ, which includes not only experiencing the joys but also the pain and suffering of the other. Moltmann himself agrees with me to a point. Beyond *Theology of Play*, he advocates for local congregations who follow Christ's example of suffering love to be willing to suffer with others in need of healing. [72] However, Moltmann's call for suffering with the marginalized clashes with his vision of play as delightful or mirthful. His political commitments are mismatched with his doxological theology of play. In revising his work on playing, I argue for a broader understanding to playing that can include not only joyful relating but also empathically suffering with one another. A richer understanding of being-with/for-one another provides a more complex way of understanding playing as Easter life.

---

70. Informal conversation with Laura Ruth Jarrett, adapted from Episcopal Church, "Collect."

71. Moltmann, *Theology of Play*, 2.

72. Moltmann, "Diaconal Church," 28–29.

The third major event in Christian history that Moltmann anticipates is the fulfillment of God's kingdom. In *Theology of Play*, he argues that Christians are to play in joyous response to the resurrection, but here too Moltmann's thinking developed elsewhere suggests that in a revision of his work playing might be understood as part of the "process of resurrection." Moltmann writes: "In talking about Christ's resurrection we have therefore to talk about a *process of resurrection*. This process has its foundation in Christ, its dynamic in the Spirit, and its future in the bodily new creation of all things."[73] Resurrection is "not what was once done, but what is in the making: the transition from death to life."[74]

Moltmann's notion that the resurrection is ongoing resonates with my proposal that revelatory experiencing is related to revelation. Christ's revelation at the cross may have been a historic event, but the wisdom of it continues to emerge in the everyday events of revelatory experiencing. They are part of the "process of resurrection," in Moltmann's words. He affirms that participating in the process of resurrection "means participating in the creative act of God."[75] From his early volume on play, one recalls that playing is part of God's creativity, as it was in the creation of the world, and as it was in the resurrection itself. In Moltmann revised, it follows that playing is participation in the ongoing process of resurrection—participating in what is life giving.

Moltmann has in mind that playing anticipates the kingdom of God, but his other work suggests that he also understands the Spirit's role in preparing for what is to come. He writes, "[T]he kingdom of glory does not come unexpectedly and without any preparation, it is already heralded in the kingdom of the Spirit, where it already has power and is present."[76] In extending Moltmann's original work on play, one might conclude that we are living in the "kingdom of the Spirit" and that in our playing we lean into the "kingdom of glory."

In Moltmann revised, the notion of "leaning into" God's new creation builds on his thinking about games as "counter-environments." In *Theology of Play*, playing is resistance against a world of injustice and pain, allowing Christians to come to know an alternative future, giving them hope for the kingdom or God's new creation (Moltmann proposes translating the Greek

73. Moltmann, *Way of Jesus Christ*, 240–41.

74. Ibid.

75. Ibid.

76. Moltmann, *Source of Life*, 11.

for "kingdom of God" into "the new creation."[77]) In my view, Christians are to lean into God's new creation. Where there is greatest suffering and brokenness, Christians are to play the most, bringing what is life-giving to places of death. Building on Moltmann, I would argue that neither human playing nor leaning into what is to come is the once-and-for-all revelation of Easter. Rather, both invite the faithful to live into what is revelatory.

From re-weaving Moltmann's work, we pull forward two key threads for our discussion of revelatory experiencing in light of playing. First, *in the fullness of playing together through experiences of both delight and suffering, we help to usher in God's new creation.* Being-with/for-others in playing, we embody wisdom and hope that is experienced as revelatory. Left alone, we cannot muster new, life-giving hope, but only with and because of others do we experience what is deeply needed. We also pull forward a second thread from Moltmann revised: *Love is the basis for God and humans playing together.* Moltmann revised gives us a lens to see in the biblical text examples of humans and Spirit playing for love's sake. In what follows, some biblical exegesis fills out a fuller vision of how Spirit's passionate seeking coincides with the vulnerability of human longing, expressed in seeking and finding Spirit. Familiar, ancient stories become fresh, illustrating why revelation and revelatory experiencing (then and now) are transformative and powerful.

HIDE-AND-SEEK WITH THE HOLY SPIRIT

An important metaphor for Christian life is the play of love, in which human beings play hide-and-seek with the Holy Spirit.[78] Out of the soul's intense longing for God, believers dedicate themselves to seeking Spirit, which never ceases to seek the beloved. Nowhere is the metaphor of hide-and-seek more poetically expressed than in the Song of Songs. Representing God and the human soul, each part takes turns longing for and seeking the hidden other. He pleads, "O my dove, in the clefts of the rock, in the covert of the cliff, let me see your face, let me hear your voice; for your voice is sweet, and your face is lovely."[79] In turn she laments, "Upon my bed at night I sought him whom my soul loves; I sought him, but found

77. Moltmann, *Way of Jesus Christ*, 98.

78. Ulanov, *Finding Space*, 16–17.

79. Song of Songs 2:14.

him not; I called him, but he gave no answer."[80] She searches the city streets, asking the watchmen if they have seen her beloved. When she finds him, she will not let him go. There is faithfulness in continuing to search for the beloved other, even when he or she is hidden from perception. The Song of Songs encourages the faithful to trust the mutuality of humanity's relationship with God. The soul is seeking God, and God is seeking the soul even as the other is obscured.

In longing for God, human beings reach for the divine through the senses. Human capacity to perceive the divine may be limited but it is heightened in the experience of playing. For in playing, the ordinary senses can soften, melt, and give way to the "spiritual senses" as the so-called "real world" drops away temporarily and players enter a world "as if." The notion of spiritual senses can be traced to the early church. Origen believed that after the Fall, humanity retained some of the rich capacity to perceive God through the senses, though this capacity was greatly diminished from what it once was.[81] Recognizing the need to strengthen the spiritual senses, Ignatius of Loyola developed spiritual exercises to attune the senses to perceive divine mystery.[82] Ignatian spiritual exercises summon one's ability to see, feel, smell, and sometimes taste what is described in the biblical text as if one were there. This and other practices that invite playing nurture the ability to perceive what is deep within or behind what registers to the ordinary senses.

The Hebrew Bible describes the Holy Spirit as *ruach*, meaning "breath" or "wind." In the story of Genesis, God sends the wind over the earth to calm the waters and God's breath brings the first human to life.[83] Sensing Spirit in wind and breath, writers of the Hebrew Bible call upon *yetzer* or the "imagination of the heart."[84] Although it can be inclined toward good or evil, at its best *yetzer* leads to the heart's imaginative knowing that interprets sense data in light of God's goodness.[85] Ideally, *yetzer* allows the spiritual seeker to draw nearer to God and to participate in Spirit's creative acts.[86] Behind the imagination of the heart, there is longing to experience

---

80. Song of Songs 3:1.

81. García-Rivera, *Community of the Beautiful*, 172.

82. Ibid., 173.

83. Genesis 1:2 and 2:7.

84. García-Rivera, *Community of the Beautiful*, 176.

85. Ibid.

86. Ibid., 180.

God with all of one's senses. God is partly known in the familiar yet beyond what human imagination can envision. In describing Spirit as *ruach*, writers of the Hebrew Bible invite readers to perceive the unpredictable nature of Spirit as well as its role in empowering and guiding the faithful.[87]

Despite the longing of faithful hearts to see God face to face, there is also the human tendency to hide from God and from conscious knowing. An archetypal image is Adam and Eve hiding from God after eating from the Tree of Knowledge. Ashamed, the couple hide in order to avoid trouble with God, but in effect they turn away from being children of God. God must go looking for the missing couple, calling out for them.[88] Traditionally, the story emphasizes the sin of eating forbidden fruit, pinning guilt on the first couple. Taken more broadly, the biblical text attests to the way that (regardless of whose fault it is) brokenness of the world results in hiding. The story reveals human nature as sensitive to judgment and disapproval. Faced with the prospect of being exposed and seen as unacceptable, the human tendency is to hide from God, self, and others.

Israel is the story of a people in hiding, being sought by God, and in being found becoming part of God's new creation. They run not only from their enemies but sometimes from God's will and their destiny as God's people. Von Balthasar observes that being God's chosen (sought out), the Israelites forget that that they have been in the process of seeking God. In other words, the grace of being found (i.e., being chosen) is soon forgotten.[89] However, I argue that like a faithful lover, God is determined to seek and find Israel. Being reconciled and reunited with God promises transformation into greater joy. God commands Ezekiel to say to Israel, "A new heart I will give you, and a new spirit [*ruach*] I will put within you; and I will remove from your body the heart of stone and give you a heart of flesh. I will put my spirit within you, and make you follow my statutes and be careful to observe my ordinances."[90] The language used by the prophet resonates with the Genesis account of creation, suggesting that the restoration of Israel will be like a new creation.[91] In addition, the passage suggests that the divine Spirit is the source of life as God's Spirit is lived in the

---

87. Averbeck, "Breath," 36–37.

88. Genesis 3:8–9.

89. von Balthasar, *Creator Spirit*, 319–20.

90. Ezekiel 36:26–27.

91. Morales, *Restoration*, 33.

human person.[92] The text poignantly describes a people so estranged from life in God that they have hearts of stone, like the way vitality shrivels up in those who cannot live authentically. However, God offers the grace of Spirit, which fills the beloved with a sense of hope in transformed living. The hiding human can be healed by the creativity and liveliness of Spirit.

As God's beloved, the faithful are to be "found" by the Holy Spirit so that they can participate in helping to bring forth abundant possibilities for all creation. Humanity is meant to participate in Spirit's mysterious creativity that sustains the world and animates physical life. The prophet Ezekiel stood with God before a valley of dry bones.[93] By God's command, he called forth the breath of life to enter the bones. Given skin, flesh, and muscle, the bones transformed into human bodies able to leap, run, and jump with grace. The story represents a divine-human partnership of creativity, in which the human prophet was guided and empowered by Spirit. Like the earlier new heart passage, the dry bones narrative harkens back to the God of Genesis.[94] It too suggests the creator God (in the form of Spirit) is at the heart of re-creating. God told Ezekiel that the bones were the people of Israel, who needed to be reconciled with the future that God intended.

In the story of the dry bones, the roles of active seeking and waiting to be found both describe humanity. Human beings are the wandering Isarelites in need of being found and experiencing transformation. At the same time, the faithful are called to be prophets like Ezekiel, invited to participate in the Spirit's seeking, finding, and calling forth those who feel dead or are in hiding. Christians who are "saved" commit to seeking and finding the souls who hide themselves from God. However, in every person there exists parts of self that are actively seeking Spirit even as there are others that are in hiding, waiting to be loved and transformed.

In partnership with the Holy Spirit, Jesus was constantly drawing out and loving the marginalized and the oppressed, those who were forced into hiding because they were despised by the dominant society. One such story is Jesus' encounter with a Samaritan woman at the well.[95] By speaking to her and asking for a drink of water, Jesus takes the woman by surprise. Not only is he speaking to a woman, he is speaking to a Samaritan, and allowing himself to become ritually unclean by drinking from her cup. She

92. Averbeck, "Breath," 36; Moltmann, *Spirit of Life*, 56.

93. Ezekiel 37:1–14.

94. Morales, *Restoration*, 34.

95. John 4:1–40.

is filled with wonder as Jesus reveals knowledge that a stranger would not know about her. In doing so, Jesus invites her into playing in God's new creation, where truth is revealed mysteriously. This is a moment in a world "as if," where the kingdom of heaven briefly meets earthly life. Jesus tells the woman that she has had five husbands and that the man she is living with is not her husband. She has likely hidden this history from others since it would be have been considered shameful. At this point, Jesus captivates her, especially when he admits to being the Messiah. She responds to his gift by telling others of the miraculous knowledge he revealed to her. She must tell others because she has become a new creation.

Jesus' life and ministry were inextricably intertwined with the hide-and-seek play of Spirit. He called upon the Holy Spirit to heal the sick and raise the dead, allowing them to live into a grace-filled world of possibilities. He was so fully one with Spirit that his every act was creative, transformative, and not fully predictable.[96] In playing, he coaxed people into trading hearts of stone for hearts of flesh. When Jesus played, he facilitated experiences of revelation, but when human beings encounter Spirit in the hide-and-seek of revelatory experiencing, we discover in small doses what it must have been like to experience the playing of Jesus. Jesus' playing with those in need of healing and liberation exemplifies a wider understanding of playing that that can include but also moves beyond Moltmman's vision of play as joyous, lighthearted, and mirthful.

The metaphor of Spirit playing speaks accurately of Spirit's creativity, fervor, and ability to give life. It also connotes Spirit's ability to generate endless possibilities and to recruit the faithful into participating in them.[97] The play of Spirit is surprising, wondrous, and not fully knowable. However, the play of Spirit somehow includes humanity and all of creation in becoming new. Out of God's love, human beings are sought after in the play of Spirit. In the slow process of human becoming, the Spirit of God waits. Moltmann writes that God waits, not in a passive sense but with keen interest in God's beloved. "Waiting means expecting, expecting means inviting, inviting means attracting, alluring, and enticing. By doing this, the waiting

---

96. Moltmann, *Way of Jesus Christ*, 94–95; Moltmann, *History and the Triune God*, 84.

97. Process theology explores God as the provider of infinite possibilities. God is continually luring humanity into the most life-giving possibilities and inviting humanity into partnership in the process of co-creation.

and awaiting one keeps an open space for the other, gives the other time, and creates possibilities of life for the other."[98]

CHRISTIANS PLAYING TO SEEK, FIND, AND BE FOUND

The notion of Christian life as the play of hide-and-seek with Spirit fills in a picture of God's role in human playing, how God is playing together with humans, and how human beings respond to God. Interpreting the biblical text, one reads accounts of experiences of revelation in which God's people are playing with Spirit, participating in Spirit's creative making, and living a bit of the new creation on earth. The text can be a source for timeless wisdom in part because it addresses the basic nature of human beings to hide and at some level to want to be found.

Every day human beings hide—not because they want to, but because they feel the need for self-protection. I hide from what I fear will harm me, and I also hide things from myself because they threaten my sense of self and the world, which I need in order to feel safe. There are some hard truths (memories, emotions, and deeply held beliefs) that I unconsciously keep from myself. This is what human beings do to get by, but beyond this hiding can be normed by social structures, making it even more difficult to detect. Without even realizing it, people in the United States hide every day within the safety of various kinds of privilege that go with race, gender, sexuality, ability, and class. There are clear incentives to maintain false self that benefits from privilege. To engage in creative or spontaneous resistance against privilege is to cast oneself outside the powerful protection of what is dominant in society and what it deems to be normal and acceptable.[99] It is far easier not to know or not to see privilege rather than to live as children of God, which requires risk, response, and change. At the same time, privilege also forces into hiding those who are oppressed by privilege, but this is a different kind of hiding, which is not only self-protective but more importantly coerced. For those who have no choice but to hide, it is difficult to accept themselves as children of God. For the privileged, hiding is a defensive strategy that indicates the presence of unexamined patterns of thinking, feeling, or doing that keep individuals captive. In hiding, there is the intense desire not to be exposed, yet paradoxically for the true self,

98. Moltmann, "God's Kenosis," 149.
99. See Thandeka, *Learning to be White*.

never to be "found" is devastating.[100] To complicate matters, most people tend to be privileged in some circumstances but oppressed in others, which means they hide in some cases but not others.

In playing, the faithful not only seek the Holy Spirit, they put themselves in a position to be found by Spirit. An indication of this is when Christians confess their sins, their woundedness, and that of the world in order to be forgiven and reconciled with God and one another. They expose some of their hiding places (i.e., those that are conscious) and their habitual need to hide. In Christian ritual, the faithful are invited into a time and space apart from the "normal" routines and performances of false self. Liturgy is crafted to open up the faithful to encounter wisdom, beauty, and goodness. It can disrupt holding patterns of thinking, feeling, or doing by allowing the faithful to imagine alternative futures and to sense new ways of being. It can invite true self to respond spontaneously and authentically to surprise, wonder, and fresh possibilities. Even if playing at church is temporary, when individuals emerge it is more difficult to return to hiding in exactly the same way. Playing "as if" facilitates the perception of the spiritually true.[101] Within each person are countless reasons to hide from God or conscious knowing and thus from one another. Hiding and being found by Spirit happens again and again in a slow process of liberation.

Seeking, finding, and being found by Spirit in our lives with one another is how we lean into God's new creation. This brings greater specificity to Moltmann's notion of being-with/for-one-another. The process of seeking, finding, and being found is carried out with one another for love's sake—not only with people like us or whom we like but all of God's people. Being able to experience the authenticity of people's joys and their suffering is vital to experiencing what is revelatory. Spirit reveals and transforms in the midst of the encounter.

100. Winnicott, *Maturational Processes*, 186.

101. Miller, *God and Games*, 145.

chapter 4

PLAYING HISTORICALLY:
MEDIEVAL PRACTICES

Having situated playing within psychoanalytic and theological frameworks, we need a historical point of reference to continue deepening understanding of Christians playing. This I approach modestly, using examples from medieval Christianity as mini-case studies. However, it is important to keep in mind that retrieving playing from Christian history is a contemporary project. Only since the modern era has playing been understood and studied as a category of human behavior. However, from the beginning of Christian faith, believers have been formed by revelatory experiencing, which can be understood in terms of playing. Some of the most creative examples of Christians playing can be found in the Middle Ages.

During medieval church history, practices of religious devotion were intended to engage the whole person—not only the rational mind but also the emotions, the imagination, and the body.[1] Especially in the medieval monastic tradition of the West, the whole person was cultivated through a life of worship, work, and study. In the Benedictine community, "[a] novice was initiated into the community through a kind of practical process of imagination, an exercise of both the creative faculty of the mind and the mnemonic capacity of the physical body."[2] All aspects of Benedictine life were intended to form the novice by evoking memory, including words and images of the biblical text as well as bodily movement in worship and prayer.[3] In the medieval era, people believed that in order for human be-

1. Hamburger, *Visual and the Visionary*, 19.
2. Neville, "Monastic Imagination?"
3. Ibid.

ings to know or remember, they must see an image, upon which the mind could build thoughts or prayers.[4] While some held a positive view of imagination, others held more negative or ambivalent views of imagination, which are discussed below. Nevertheless, the holistic approach to Christian formation in medieval monasticism created hospitality for practices that fostered revelatory experiencing.

As in contemporary contexts, revelatory experiencing in the medieval era was understood as playing neither by practitioners nor by church authorities. In fact, many would have denied strongly that playing was related to experiencing Christ; they would have associated playing only with childishness, frivolity, and entertainment. In medieval times, the faithful had their own ways of describing their experience, just as every generation of Christians has. Nothing can detract from the importance of their emic understanding of what I am calling revelatory experiencing. However, theological and psychoanalytic perspectives on playing provide lenses for exploring what was perhaps taken for granted by the practitioners themselves and overlooked by others.

Examples of medieval Christians playing reveal how revelatory experiencing deepened Christian formation and allowed the faithful to be—as Moltmann says—with/for those who were marginalized, alienated, or oppressed. At the same time, the playing of "saints" (broadly understood) offers new insights on a theory of facilitating revelatory experiencing. Playing with devotional dolls and holy fools serve as two examples that provide opportunities for mutually critical dialogue among these historic practices, Winnicott's theory of playing, Moltmann, and other theological reflections on playing.

PLAYING WITH DEVOTIONAL DOLLS

In the fourteenth century, nuns in the Rheinland, Germany, played with dolls as a practice of venerating the infant Jesus. Not only do descriptions of these devotional dolls exist, some of the dolls and their accessories have survived.[5] A small trove of these treasures belongs to the Cistercian convent of the Holy Cross in Rostock in northeastern Germany, which owns as many as seven "*Poppen*" or in modern German "*Puppen*" or dolls. One example is "*Christ Child*," imported from Mechelen in the Lower Countries,

4. Carruthers, *Craft of Thought*, 69–73.
5. Hamburger, *Visual and the Visionary*, 23.

which was housed in the center of a reliquary shrine. The shrine appears to give easy access to the doll, suggesting that the doll was meant to be handled and not merely seen.[6] The dolls are part of the convent's collection of other devotional dolls and accessories including *"Zwey kleine Poppen wieg"* or "two small dolls' cradles" and a Madonna and Child dating to the thirteenth century.[7]

For the Madonna and Child, the nuns sewed an elaborate wardrobe made from Italian silk that includes three sets of clothing for Mary and one for the baby Jesus. Mary wears an intricate crown that was one of eighteen such crowns once in the nuns' possession.[8] The existence of the miniature clothes and accessories suggests that dressing the dolls was an important practice. Dressing the dolls in finery endowed them with bodies and made them more lifelike.[9] Rather than being an object to admire from a distance, the dolls "cry out to be dressed, undressed, caressed, and consoled."[10] In other words, the doll begged for relationship in needing to be attended to, much like a real child. As in play with any doll, the figure of Jesus or Mary came to life in creative ways when dressed, undressed, and held.

Little is known about how the nuns understood practices related to the dolls, though the artifacts suggest they were used to enact reverence for Mary and the Christ child. It is reasonable to assume that the practice was communal if contemporary Carmelite practices with the Infant of Prague (discussed below) are linked to the play of the Rheinland nuns. Although the nuns would not have called their devotional practice "playing," the notion of playing helps to illumine the practice. One can imagine that the practice invited revelatory experiencing for various reasons.

First, the dolls allowed the sisters to seek and "find" the Christ child and his mother, playing at/in the new creation by using their creativity, imagination, and senses. One can imagine that one purpose of this was to lose themselves in this contemplative practice in order to live more fully into a world of possibilities created by these sacred objects. By practicing devotion to Mary and the Christ child, the nuns were placing themselves in a position to be "found" by the Holy Spirit. They were practicing humble,

6. Ibid.

7. Ibid.

8. Ibid

9. Ibid.

10. Ibid.

spiritual availability—consistently "showing up" and being open to encountering divine mystery.

Playing with devotional dolls invited the nuns to act and believe "as if" the baby Jesus and Mary were alive. This is no different than Christians today going out on a "date night" with Jesus or going on a "walk" with God to develop a closer relationship with God.[11] Acting as if God were a real person is a practice that makes divine reality more accessible and believable to some Christians. The difference here is that the dolls provided a tangible focal point for creativity, imagination, and the senses. At some level, the nuns must have been aware that the dolls were not living or divine even if they were sacred. Otherwise they would have been committing idolatry.

By playing, the nuns could seek and "find" Jesus by enacting their devotion for him through expressions of motherly attentiveness to and care for the doll. The practice also allowed the sisters to seek and "find" Mary, helping them to identify more closely with the Virgin. The same intimate knowledge of Mary could not be achieved by simply reading about her, talking about her, or even praying to her. Rather, there was power in dramatizing or performing a relationship with her that made Mary more present, tangible, and more real. At times her realness was likely experienced as life-giving. To play with devotional dolls was to wonder at the miracle of God taking human form and at the remarkable role that Mary played in the redemption of humanity. More generally, the dolls invited wonder at the miracle of creating human life and the special role that all women play in it. The seeking and finding of Mary and Jesus, playing "as if " they were alive, and being filled with wonder by the nativity—all of these are suggestive of revelatory experiencing.

Second, the Rheinland nuns' practice may have fostered revelatory experiencing by helping them to claim their faith as women religious. Visual art of the same period suggests that playing with dolls was part of a larger repertoire of devotional practices that appealed to maternal feelings. One can imagine that these practices allowed the nuns to sense obliquely what was missing from their lives—the loving intimacy between mother and child. A statuette entitled "Maria Rocks Baby Jesus," which originates from the Upper Rhein of Germany, circa 1350–1375, depicts the infant Christ sitting in his cradle, stretching out his arms to Mary as if wanting to nurse.[12] The scene expresses the everydayness of Mary's motherhood,

11. Luhrmann, *When God Talks Back*, 80.

12. Little, *Krone und Schleier*, 455.

which any woman of faith might appreciate. This statuette (and others like it) allowed the nuns to contemplate the "physical motherhood [of Mary] which the nuns have been denied."[13] In light of this, play with devotional dolls seems poignant and understandable.

The dolls must also be understood in the context of women mystics of the time, who experienced revelations having to do with the baby Jesus or with Mary and motherhood. For example, Gertrude of Helfta (1256 – ca. 1302) had mystical visions of clasping the newborn Jesus to her own breast in love and devotion.[14] At one point in her spiritual journey, she envisioned Mary asking her to give the infant back, looking at Gertrude with disapproval for not taking proper care of Jesus.[15] Naturally, the saint was filled with remorse and asked the Virgin for forgiveness. Female mystic Margaretha Ebner (1291–1351) received "motherhood visions," after she received a "Jesus cradle" gift from Vienna in 1344.[16] Birgitta of Sweden (1303-1373), who was a mother of eight, identified with Mary as a holy womb that brought God's word into the world.[17] She experienced herself as a vessel for God's revelations, dedicating herself to producing spiritual children of God through her teaching and writing.[18] The experiences of these women mystics help us to understand playing with devotional dolls as potentially revelatory.

Playing with devotional dolls was likely revelatory at times in that it also allowed the nuns to play creatively with God images. On one hand, the sisters played with images of the Christ child that were given by tradition. These God images provided by Christian tradition are "objective object-images" of God.[19] On the other hand, the nuns brought to this practice of dolls their personal images of God. They imagined Jesus as a human baby that needed to be held, cuddled, and cared for by a loving mother. This was not only the Christ child given by tradition, but also *their* baby Jesus constructed in their imagination and expressed creatively in the dolls. These intimate images of Christ were "subjective object images" of God, which come from people's lives and are vital to making God feel tangible

13. Ibid.

14. Gertrude, *Gertrude of Helfta*, 115.

15. Ibid., 116.

16. Little, *Krone und Schleier*, 455.

17. Stjerna, "Birgitta of Sweden," 135.

18. Ibid., 136.

19. Ulanov, *Finding Space*, 30.

and believable to people.[20] Play with these devotional dolls took place in the creative space between objective and subjective images of God, which serve to correct and balance one another.[21]

Though the practice of devotional dolls likely facilitated revelatory experiencing, the practice was easily misunderstood. Later critics scoffed at the imagery used by nuns in their devotions. In 1785, an anonymous contributor to the *Freymüthige* or *Freethinker* wrote, "The female imagination is always more sensitive than the male imagination and, therefore, at least in an isolated existence accompanied by continuous introspection, open to every kind of foolishness."[22] Pointing to the images used by nuns in their devotions, the writer goes on, "The female sex has a natural, irresistible inclination to be with children. If there are no living children at hand, then they make them out of wood or rags. Even at the age of fifty, the nun remains herself a child who plays with a holy doll just like a three-year-old girl with a secular effigy."[23] This distorted account of the nuns' spirituality suggests that the practice of devotional dolls was misunderstood to some degree by the wider culture as well as other parts of the church.

Devotional images used by nuns in late medieval Christianity were routinely trivialized and treated with suspicion because of their physicality,[24] suggesting that the nuns were marginalized in a monastic culture dominated by men. There were often tensions between female nuns and the men who supervised their spiritual development, who were wary of the power of devotional imagery to provide an imaginative escape for the senses.[25] While medieval devotion involved the whole person, including the body, sensual engagement was to be highly controlled. The use of dolls, a devotional practice for women by women, suggests resistance against the marginalization of female spirituality.

Those who dismissed the significance of the dolls and other devotional images were partly following an older Christian tradition of suspicion of towards images of the divine, which was in tension with more positive understandings of imagination in Christian formation. Early Church Fathers wrote scathingly against the making and use of images and representational

---

20. Ibid., 23.

21. Ibid., 23, 26–27.

22. Hamburger, *Visual and the Visionary*, 22.

23. Ibid.

24. Ibid., 24.

25. Ibid., 19.

art. Justin Martyr condemned as blasphemous and corrupt the work of artisans who made objects for worship. He urged the faithful to be led by virtue and the intellect instead of falling prey to idolatry.[26] Lactantius (c. 240–320) argued that the foolish create and worship images that are "dead" likenesses of God, rather than seeking the living God.[27] These concerns point to the inherent slipperiness of images, their capacity to draw in the faithful, and their power to evoke imagination. Iconoclastic views express legitimate nervousness about the effect of images on faith formation because they are not easy to predict and impossible to control. Understandably, for some the safest route was simply to reject images. However, some church thinkers recognized that something vital to faith would be lost with the banning of devotional images. The Second Council of Nicaea (787) declared representational art "in harmony with the history of the spread of the gospel, as it provides confirmation that the becoming of man in the Word of God was real and not just imaginary, and as it brings us a similar benefit."[28] It is striking that the Council recognized that devotional images helped Jesus feel real to the faithful, thereby making faith feel real.

To unsympathetic eyes, the *Puppen* could be seen as a danger or be minimized as "just a doll" or "just an object."[29] Seeing an object as a "nothing"[30] is to see the world with an "arrogant eye," which positions oneself over and against the object to be known and keeps it at a distance.[31] However, to see nothing more than "just a doll" forecloses revelatory experiencing, which decenters and renegotiates pre-conceived categories and relationships, including relationships with "things." Rather than the doll remaining an "it" to be acted upon, the nuns saw the doll as a "Thou" who could act upon the faithful by evoking creative imagination and being a conduit of grace.[32] This required a "loving eye," willing to see the dolls with sympathy and openness.[33] Acting as if the dolls were little people involved shifting into a mode of relationship that opened up transformative possi-

---

26. Justin, "Justin Martyr," 44–45.

27. Ibid., 45.

28. Ibid., 64.

29. For Christian relationships with everyday objects, see Stephen Pattison, *Seeing Things*.

30. O'Brien, *A Cry of Stone*.

31. McFague, *Super, Natural Christians*, 88–90

32. Buber, *I and Thou*.

33. McFague, *Super, Natural Christians*, 112–17.

bilities. Relating subject-to-subject, playing with dolls was like playing with a real person who could respond.

When many convents were dissolved in the early modern period, much of the devotional imagery of nuns did not meet Renaissance notions of "fine art" and therefore was deemed unworthy of preservation.[34] There could have been many more dolls such as those kept by the Rheinland nuns. No doubt they suffered a larger trend toward the "suppression, misrepresentation, and obliteration" of the visual culture of female monasticism in the Middle Ages.[35] In addition, it was all too convenient to forget what appeared to be the foolish playing of monastic women. However, the practice of playing with devotional dolls was compelling enough that it resurfaced elsewhere at a later time.

In 1628, Polyxena of Lobkowicz bequeathed a Christ child doll to Our Lady of Victory Church in Prague. The doll was a wedding gift to Polyxena's mother, the Duchess Maria Manrique de Lara, who inherited the doll from her mother. According to one legend, the doll belonged to Saint Theresa of Avila, who was passionately devoted to the Christ child.[36] The Infant of Prague, as the doll is known, is venerated throughout the world. At Our Lady of Victory, Carmelite sisters dress the Infant, much like the Rheinland nuns cared for their dolls. In Prague, the church has acquired approximately one hundred costumes for the divine child, most of which are gifts of devotion and thanksgiving.[37] Those who care for the Infant of Prague understand that dressing the figure "is intended to bring Jesus closer to the faithful as a real human being. It helps us to experience the closeness of Jesus and to express our love and reverence."[38] Our Lady of Victory traces the veneration of the Infant to the early fourteenth century. "The oldest statues come from Germany and are probably connected with the visionary milieu in female convents."[39] One can thus trace a lineage between the Rheinland nuns playing with *Puppen* and contemporary Christians playing with the Infant of Prague.

---

34. Hamburger, *Visual and the Visionary*, 14.

35. Ibid., 15.

36. Monastery of the Infant Jesus of Prague, "History."

37. Monastery of the Infant Jesus of Prague, "Robes."

38. Ibid.

39. Monastery of the Infant Jesus of Prague, "Veneration."

PLAYING BY PRETENSE: HOLY FOOLS

A second example of medieval Christians playing was holy foolery. Interestingly, this example stretches the imagination to consider that playing takes various and unexpected forms. Playing with devotional dolls might seem more like what we commonly regard as playing. One can imagine tenderness in the playing of the Rheinland nuns and perhaps sweetness and joy in mothering. However, playing looks and feels different in the context of fools for Christ, who evoked a range of emotions, including dedication, scorn, and mirth. The playing of holy fools broadens our understanding not only of playing being carried out in surprising activities but also of revelatory experiencing encompassing a variety of feelings.

Holy fools were Christians who simulated folly in response to the call of the Holy Spirit to live into a vocation.[40] In a sense, holy fools were deliberately playing by pretense. They created and lived in a world "as if" they were Christ, calling people to a more godly way of life. They pretended to be insane, gave up their wealth, never set down roots, and called into question so-called wise and worldly ways.[41] They modeled themselves on Christ's humility, poverty, and experience of being ridiculed. In France, Louise de Neant (b. 1639) was treated as a screaming madwoman possessed by the devil. In the Salpêtrière, she was thrown into a rat-infested dungeon and suffered from contagious sores. After receiving absolution and Holy Communion, Louise was healed in mind and body. From then she simulated madness as a means of growing in humility and conformity to Christ.[42]

Not only did holy fools exist in a rich tradition of hagiography (biographies of the saints), radical Orthodox and Catholics also took up holy fool behavior in everyday life. While some of the holy fools in hagiography are blended accounts of people, they were based on the acts of real people. On one occasion Saint Francis of Assisi (1181/2–1226 CE) and Brother Ruffino stood at the pulpit naked and were mocked by people, who thought they "had gone mad out of an excess of penance."[43] However, when Francis preached on the nakedness and humiliation of Christ, they wept with remorse. Francis facilitated revelatory experiencing that caught his followers

---

40. Saward, *Perfect Fools*, 25. For holy fools in multiple religious traditions, see Phan, "Wisdom of Holy Fools," 740–42; Otto, *Fools Are Everywhere*.

41. Saward, *Perfect Fools*, 25–30.

42. Ibid., 176–77.

43. Hughes, *Little Flowers*, 107–8. Cited in Saward, *Perfect Fools*, 85.

by surprise. Not only did they glimpse Christ in Saint Francis, they also became aware of the ugly side of human nature that would humiliate another.

Most but not all fools for Christ were monastics in the Orthodox and Roman Catholic traditions. The heyday of holy fools began in the thirteenth century and ended in the sixteenth, reaching its height in the fifteenth and early sixteenth centuries.[44] Holy foolishness in Russia enjoyed its golden age from the fifteenth to the first half of the seventeenth century.[45] The playing of holy fools can be traced from the apostle Paul to saints in Byzantium, Western Europe, and Russia.

Paul was the first "fool for Christ."[46] Although many accused him of madness, Paul uses the word *mōros* to refer to himself as a fool for Christ's sake.[47] In its common usage, *mōros* indicates real insanity, but Paul recognizes that what appears to be madness can be a guise for the mysterious truth of the Gospel.[48] He argues that unlike worldly wisdom, which seeks power and fortune, in God's wisdom God speaks through what is weak.[49] By worldly standards, Christ's sacrifice is folly, but Paul makes the same critique of so-called "wisdom of the world."[50] According to Paul, habitual human ways of being in the world—arrogance, self-deception, and self-righteousness—are so contrary to God's being that they need to be challenged. The drastic measures of holy fools speak to their conviction of how deeply entrenched their fellow human beings were in worldly values. Describing the phenomenon of holy foolery as playing illumines how these Christians used radical creativity to facilitate revelatory experiencing, destabilizing what was taken for granted in order for the faithful to embrace more life-giving possibilities.

Some holy fools inspired laughter of wonder and delight. This light-hearted expression of holy foolery resembles the playing of the Rheinland nuns in practicing wonder and joy at the nativity. In the West, holy fools excelled at drawing people out and coaxing them into play with humor, storytelling, or song. These mirthful holy fools should not be confused with jesters who served in clerical contexts of medieval Europe, whose function

44. Saward, *Perfect Fools*, 80.

45. Panchenko, "Laughter as Spectacle," 42.

46. 1 Corinthians 4:10.

47. Acts 17:32 and Acts 26:24; Saward, *Perfect Fools*, 5.

48. Ibid.

49. 1 Corinthians 1:26–30.

50. 1 Corinthians 1:20; Saward, *Perfect Fools*, 3.

was to mock the proud and the corrupt.[51] Unlike the holy fools, jesters operated in the open. Saint Francis called his disciples to be "jongleurs of the Lord" [*joculatores Domini*], preaching, singing praise, and moving the hearts of the people to spiritual joy.[52] In the Western Catholic tradition, holy foolery celebrated mirth.[53] St. Philip Neri (1515–59) was known for constantly telling jokes, performing silly dances in front of cardinals, or wearing his clothes in ridiculous ways. He used to make people laugh by taking hold of someone by the chin, hair, or beard.[54] Those who met him did not know his austere asceticism or his intent to bring scorn upon himself in order to remain humble.[55]

In the mirthful playing of holy fools, saints were creating conditions that invited people to respond spontaneously and to "go with" playing, so that they might experience much-needed spiritual wisdom. In this approach, the holy fools sought to draw out the faithful—to forget momentarily their "adult" roles, pretenses, and protective guises—in order to become lost yet found in experiencing greater spiritual aliveness. Similarly, one can imagine the Rheinland nuns having to set aside some adult knowing (e.g., knowledge of the crucifixion) in order to become lost in holding the Christ child. In either case, only then could the faithful experience playing. Being caught up in the playing of holy fools (or the dolls of the Rheinland nuns) helped the faithful to become aware of themselves as children of God (and probably their resistance to living as children of God). Like the nuns, some holy fools in the Catholic West modeled what it looks like to act and respond creatively and spontaneously in love, trust, and joy.

Some scholars of holy foolery, especially from the east, discount the light-hearted holy foolery of the Western Catholic tradition. While A. M. Panchenko acknowledges that Russia inherited the holy fool tradition through hagiography from Byzantium, he believes that the tradition of holy foolishness is more significant in Russia than in Byzantium or in Western Europe. For example, Panchenko would be critical of claims that holy fools flourished in Western Europe, since he claims that St. Francis of Assisi is "practically the only ascetic from the Roman Catholic world who bears a

---

51. Otto, *Fools are Everywhere*, 175.

52. Francis of Assisi, *Le Speculum perfectionis*, 274c; English translation: Sherley-Price, *St. Francis of Assisi*, 274f. Cited in Saward, *Perfect Fools*, 87.

53. Saward, *Perfect Fools*, 95.

54. Ibid., 97–98; Otto, *Fools Are Everywhere*, 169–70.

55. Saward, *Perfect Fools*, 98.

hint of resemblance to the Eastern Orthodox fool for Christ."[56] Panchenko understands holy foolishness as a type of "voluntary martyrdom."[57] He would disagree that among holy fools in the later Middle Ages there is an "unselfconscious reveling in the mirth, joy, and good humor in the life of Christ."[58] While gaiety might be true of some Western holy fools, during the sixteenth and seventeenth centuries (the heyday of holy foolishness in Russia), the Orthodox Church forbade laughter because it was considered improper Christian behavior.[59] Sergey Ivanov criticizes what he calls Catholic "quasi-holy fools," believing that the humor of holy fools is gloomy not cheerful.[60]

Though controversial, I take seriously the playing of light-hearted holy fools. The critiques made by Panchencko and Ivanov focus on the question of which holy fools are the more authentic. However, from my perspective, both Western Catholic and Eastern Orthodox fools for Christ engage the faithful in revelatory experiencing—albeit through different styles of playing. Playing helps to explain what both diverse traditions of holy foolery have in common.

Fools for Christ adopted a pedagogy of playing that shares resemblances with and yet was different from the pedagogy of playing adopted by the Rheinland nuns. Holy foolery was an ascetic practice engaged for the sake of being formed in Christ-like ways and (by doing so) being in communion with God. This is not unlike the playing of the Rheinland nuns, whose pedagogy nurtured the spiritual formation of individuals in relation to Mary and the Christ child. Like the nuns, one can imagine the saints becoming lost in the performance of being fools, yet they might experience being found (experiencing themselves as capable of being Christ-like) or finding Christ in the midst of doing so.

In both Western and Eastern traditions, the playing of holy fools was a contrast to the playing of nuns with *Puppen*, with some important pedagogical differences. The playing of holy fools was public yet undercover, unlike the playing of nuns, which was sheltered by the convent but not secret. Only the saint knew that his/her foolery was a ruse until it was

---

56. Ibid., 63.

57. Ibid., 50

58. Saward, *Perfect Fools*, 80

59. Panchenko, "Laughter as Spectacle," 106.

60. Ivanov, *Byzantium*, 395.

revealed after death (e.g., by the testimony of his/her spiritual guide).[61] Living a double life, they were men or women of prayer by night, when no one would see them praying. By day they were fools, engaging people on the street or in the marketplace.[62] Unlike the nuns, the holy fools refused to contemplate Christ only in the monastery. Instead they embodied Christ's life in the everyday form, using public space as a stage.[63] One might go so far as to say that the holy fools were performing street theater, practicing the art of improvisation. The nuns' pedagogy, as far as we know, did not extend to the public or the lives of those beyond the convent.

While the pedagogy of playing adopted by the Rheinland nuns might foster familial devotion and responsibility for caring for one another, the pedagogy of playing used by holy fools was developmentally more demanding as they transformed moral awareness in the guise of everyday life. Holy fools challenged what people would rather not know about themselves and engaged them in discomfiting moral questions. The mission of holy fools was to facilitate revelatory experiencing that would disrupt the status quo so that people were drawn into acting or reacting.

The story of Onesima illustrates the demanding nature of the fools' pedagogy. Onesima was an empress who renounced her wealth, dressed in rags, and wandered in the desert for forty years, pretending to be mad.[64] She entered a monastery, where she would not speak when questioned or walk unless forced to do so. Acting as if insane, she refused to have her feet washed, ripped her clothing, stamped her feet, and shouted. When the sisters beat her and dragged her along the floor, she rejoiced in silence. After forty years, God sent a religious man, an anchorite elder, whom Onesima refused to see until the sisters beat and pulled her to him. The elder immediately recognized her as a saint and the sisters were filled with astonishment and repentance.[65] The hagiographic literature is filled with this kind of classic account of the holy fools' provocativeness. Their playing with people was unpredictable, open-ended, and sometimes threatening and subversive. Confronting people with what might be painful and difficult suggests a higher order of experiencing with one another than that with the nuns.

61. Saward, *Perfect Fools*, 25.

62. Ibid; Panchenko, "Laughter as Spectacle," 54.

63. Ibid., 56.

64. Saward, *Perfect Fools*, 59–60.

65. Ibid., 60–62.

The fools' pedagogy depended on the support of an ecclesial culture and a wider culture. In maintaining and building a hagiographic literature of holy fools, the Roman Catholic and Orthodox churches provided a structure through which the playing of holy fools could be sustained and recognized. The traditional stories of holy fools served as a far-reaching interpretive frame. Hagiography promoted a willingness among the faithful to keep holy fools alive in their religious imaginations, to see them in their midst, and to be open to their teaching even if people were caught off guard.

Thanks to a strong hagiographic tradition, the holy fools lived among people who understood their role. The holy fool was accorded high status, as people perceived the holy fool (accurately or not) as a righteous person taking on the semblance of irrationality for the sake of asceticism or pedagogy.[66] People were aware of the possibility of being in the presence of a holy fool. Furthermore, in Byzantine culture, people had a sense that the world was permeated with sanctity. They believed that the holy could reveal itself at any moment when and where one might not expect.[67] Therefore one could never be certain who was a holy fool. Belief in legends of the "secret servants of the Lord," who could appear in the guise of the worst of ordinary lay people, gave rise to later understandings and narrations of the holy fool.[68]

In Russia, the hagiographic literature was not the only frame for understanding holy foolishness. Holy foolishness (*iuordstvo*) drew on a repertoire that helped an audience interpret what a fool was saying and doing. Not only did holy fools draw from folklore's use of enigma and parable,[69] they also employed nonverbal, theatrical "gestures." These gestures were drawn from and contributed to the popular, church, and courtly cultures in which Russians lived.[70] A typical gesture of holy fools was to provoke a crowd by spitting at it and throwing rocks and mud. When a fool performed this "kinetic phrase" (*kineticheskaia fraza*), spectators could grasp its meaning because it was a classic gesture interpreted in hagiographic accounts that also resonated with popular meanings.[71]

---

66. Ivanov, *Byzantium*, 7.

67. Ibid., 43.

68. Ibid., 167.

69. Panchenko, "Laughter as Spectacle," 79.

70. Ibid., 85.

71. Ibid., 81.

Eventually holy foolery saw its demise. In the West, the demise of foolery was caused by the dissolution of monasteries in England, which sheltered the weak and foolish; the emergence of other radical theologies (e.g., extreme forms of Calvinism and Puritanism), which rejected expressions of fun or frivolity; and upheavals that altered the social and political climate of the sixteenth century.[72] In Byzantium, the decline of holy foolery was brought on by the attacks of the Turks.[73]

A PSYCHOANALYTIC PERSPECTIVE

Winnicott's theory of playing sheds light on why the practices of the Rhineland nuns and holy fools fostered revelatory experiencing. In both cases, playing allowed the faithful to navigate a range of perceptions of reality. In playing with dolls and pretending to be fools, these saints explored their inklings about God's new creation by creating it, acting and believing "as if."

As is true of playing in general, the playing of saints was a sophisticated, original weaving of an in-between experience (in what Winnicott describes as an "intermediate area of experiencing") to which "inner reality and external life contribute[d]."[74] Like all Christians, the saints experienced inner longings, images, and devotion for Christ. In order for these to be expressed, they needed a vehicle that others could also experience—a doll or the phenomenon of the fool. Winnicott would say they needed some "fragment" derived from shared reality.[75] The nuns and fools imbued their chosen medium with their deep wishes and longing for Christ, investing meaning and feeling. Playing allowed "a sample"[76] of the saints' inner commitments and visions of faith to be seen and known indirectly—to be "played out" so to speak. Yet they were also subject to revision when playing ended and began again.

One could approach the practices of nuns and fools in light of Winnicott's concepts of transitional objects and transitional phenomena. In the first case, the *Puppen* could be understood as transitional objects. The nuns adopted these beloved dolls. (Winnicott would say they were "cathected.") His theory predicts that the nuns created a Mary and Jesus in need of

72. Saward, *Perfect Fools*, 99–101.

73. Ivanov, *Byzantium*, 240.

74. Winnicott, *Playing and Reality*, 3, 19.

75. Ibid., 69.

76. Ibid.

attention and deserving of veneration. The dolls were "used" by them and thereby "destroyed," similar to the way a child destroys a toy or a client "uses" his or her analyst.[77] For Winnicott, object destruction is crucial because what the object represents "survives" and therefore becomes more real to the person playing and can be loved all the more.[78] His theory suggests that the temporary "destruction" of the dolls allowed the nun practitioner to sense anew, for example, the Jesus beyond the infant needing care. She could perceive afresh the constancy and "the more" of Christ, exceeding what human beings can imagine in playing. What one comes to know about Jesus by playing with dolls reaches toward but always falls short of the living Christ. The connections and disconnections between the "real" and the "not real" provide an expanded, richer sense of reality. These new perceptions were, in each instance, part of revelatory experiencing.

While devotional dolls might be identified as transitional objects, the practices of holy fools could be considered transitional phenomena. Just as the Rheinland nuns were dressing up the baby Jesus in their hopes and dreams, the holy fools were performing their own versions of Christ. They took Paul's notion of being a fool for Christ and enacted their own dramatic interpretations. They went to great lengths, (in the words of Winnicott) to "manipulate[e] external phenomena in the service of the dream and invest chosen external phenomena with dream meaning and feeling."[79] In this case, the "dream" refers to the longed-for, new creation, which is experienced "as if." The holy fools enacted the dream of the new creation in order for it be seen and known in part.

For those who lived in the time of holy fools, playing came by wondering, perhaps believing, and acting as if the next fool one met could be a holy fool—all of which can be thought of in terms of transitional phenomena. In the reading of hagiography, the faithful could put themselves in the place of characters whose lives were changed when the pretense of the fool gave way to the holy. Imagining oneself in the stories of holy people was a common spiritual practice in the medieval era.[80] In reading about the saints, the faithful could be privy to the secret of the fool's true identity. The hagiographic literature set the stage for them to see creatively the holy fools in their midst—to be on the lookout for Spirit embodied in everyday form.

77. Ibid., 118–23.
78. Ibid., 120–21.
79. Ibid., 69.
80. Neville, "Monastic Imagination?" 4.

One can imagine that playing with real-life holy fools involved suspense, imagination, or playing along with what might be holy foolery. If one encountered a fool and suspected he or she was a fool for Christ, one might try to detect the slippage between "not-real" and "real," hoping to glimpse anew the living Christ that the fool was pretending to be.

From a psychoanalytic perspective, the playing of holy fools and the Rheinland nuns invited revelatory experiencing because they could potentially experience being within themselves and with others as true self. In the case of holy foolery, the saints' playing with bystanders resembles Winnicott's use of the Squiggle Game, in which he engages a child in an improvisational drawing game.[81] The psychoanalyst would scribble a shape and the child would add to it, making it into a new creation; then they would trade roles. The game frees up primary processes (e.g., using dream material) and leads to helping the child in a process of self-discovery. Similarly, holy fools would create a scenario that would provoke a reaction from an audience and create from there. The bystanders' reactions would guide the interaction. Just as the Squiggle Game brought psychic material to light, the antics of holy fools unmasked the distorted habits of the worldly wise. Being in a crowd of people laughing at a fool would allow a person to feel that it was normal or acceptable to deride the weak. However, the pedagogy of holy fools, especially in Russia, led people to experience the tragic, hidden aspect of their own laughter.[82] The tactics of Russian holy fools made people aware of what needed to be decentered, including the unexamined, sinful habits of making fun of those who appeared weak, mad, or foolish. Being confronted with unflattering truth was a humbling opportunity for re-centering and experiencing true self. Probably some Christians were not able to play because they did not feel safe enough to admit why they would laugh at the foolish or the marginalized. Some might not have been able to allow themselves to be found by Christ in the encounter with holy fools. Others might have felt secure enough to be open to feeling what was challenging or surprising, leaving room to receive what was life-giving.

Whether one was playing with devotional dolls or holy fools, the playing of saints invited revelatory experiencing because they involved indirect communication, allowing true self to be known even as it was hidden, its vulnerability protected. One way of understanding this "silent" communication (as Winnicott says) is how artists play with and through art.

81. Winnicott, "Squiggle Game," 316.
82. Panchenko, "Laughter as Spectacle," 42.

Winnicott writes, "In the artist of all kinds I think one can detect an inherent dilemma, which belongs to the co-existence of two trends, the urgent need to communicate and still more urgent need not to be found."[83] An artist's never-ending task, which demands his or whole nature, is to creatively (re)present what is inside, expressing it through art.[84] This sounds like a completely open-ended task, in which an artist has complete freedom, but in fact the artist is able to express his/her creativity because of a structure for playing that provides constructive limits and resistance. The painter's work is bound by the edges of the canvas, which serves as a frame for contemplation.[85] The artistic medium and tools of paint and brushes help to determine how the artist can express experience. Likewise, when the Rhineland nuns and holy fools were playing, their devotional practices served as containers for their imagination and creativity. Potentially they could experience being true self, while retaining the requisite cover of mediated form. Like artists, the nuns and fools fabricated their own unique creations. Even those who were inspired by the lore of holy fools crafted their own versions of themselves and the fools by imagining them and acting "as if." These medieval Christians were called to a life of devotion for which they found creative form and adapted it for their own context.

When human beings exercise their creativity, it fosters a sense of aliveness in them, as being creative leads to a sense of feeling real, which can be part of revelatory experiencing. Feeling real, which means having a sense of self and of being, is essential to health.[86] When people do not feel real, they feel that they are not themselves, they are in limbo, they are nothing, or they are detached from their bodies.[87] For Christians, not feeling real might involve feeling estranged from God, going through the motions of Christian practices, or feeling numb to their own spirit and its stirrings. For the faithful, feeling real involves sensing one's being in Christ, of being children of God. The medieval saints played through creative Christian practices because it helped keep faith alive.

83. Winnicott, *Maturational Processes*, 185.

84. Ibid.

85. Milner, *Paint*, 158, 163.

86. Winnicott et al., *Home*, 25.

87. Ibid., 35.

A THEOLOGICAL PERSPECTIVE

From a theological vantage point, the playing of the Rheinland nuns and holy fools invited revelatory experiencing for a different set of reasons from those offered by a psychoanalytic perspective. Winnicott's concepts and ideas help to reveal some of the deep psychic dynamics between people playing, explaining what the faithful might seek and find in the process of experiencing together. A psychoanalytic approach also illumines why the practices of nuns and fools help the faithful to engage reality in new ways. In contrast, taking a theological perspective reveals the role of divine playing in the midst of revelatory experiencing, the mysterious telos of such encounters, and the ways that the people are formed in faith in the midst of them.

First, the saints experienced or facilitated something of God in their playing because it involved the hide-and-seek of the Holy Spirit, which is especially clear in the case of fools for Christ. Holy fools acted with the passion of those moved by the Holy Spirit. By playing by pretense (i.e., by hiding their identity), they were in some sense found by Spirit, living into their spiritual vocation. They mimicked the nature of Spirit, exercising high creativity and unpredictability in ways understood initially only by them and by God. Unlike prophets who were chosen mediums for God's power, holy fools chose their own vocation and were solely responsible for the outcome of their actions.[88] Because they were men and women who were deeply devoted to Christ, it is reasonable to imagine that before setting out on their daily mission, they prayed to be guided by the Holy Spirit in being an instrument of transformation. It was likely that holy fools opened themselves to the creativity and grace of Spirit in the moment of performing their sacred improvisations, which sustained them while suffering humiliation, poverty, and scorn.

Second, both fools and the Rheinland nuns were creating conditions for revelatory experiencing as they engaged reality "as if" for Christ's sake—that is for the sake of love. On one level, the nuns were enacting the love and trust that bonds mother (caregiver) and child. At the same time, this is the very love and trust that faith calls humanity to have in relationship to God. In pretending to be surrogate mothers to the baby Jesus, the sisters were playing and growing more mature in faith, allowing them to

---

88. Ivanov, *Byzantium*, 13.

sense themselves as God's beloved. Beyond the form of Jesus as an innocent child was also the knowledge of Christ's sacrificial love.

Likewise, the holy fools were also playing for love's sake, suffering humiliation and marginalization because Christ sacrificed himself out of love for humanity. Engaging in holy foolery was a means of growing in relationship to the living Christ, who continues to love the world through Spirit. The true mission of holy fools was held in secret so that attention would not be focused on the person they were but on the loving, subversive role they were playing. The practice reveals a surprising connection between loving and being subversive, which would be an accurate way of describing Christ's ministry. The practice of holy foolery also highlights the sacrificial nature of love, which was also true to Christ.

Third, in their playing medieval Christians invited revelatory experiencing by leaning into God's new creation. Through playing they were creating Moltmann's notion of an "anti-environment" or a "counter-environment" that allowed them to live into new ways of being. The nuns were inhabiting a world in which both Mary and the baby Jesus were real people with whom to have relationships. The holy fools were helping people to play with a more liberating future in order to explore it and to claim it.[89] They gave others the opportunity to be with/for the marginalized, alienated, or oppressed. Like Ezekiel breathing life into dry bones, holy fools attempted to awaken people (including themselves) from deadening habits of thinking, feeling, and doing.

In addition, the nuns and fools were also creating a "counter-environment" that challenged the medieval church. Recall the classic narrative of Oneisma, in which nuns treated the fool with scorn and humiliation. The false pride and preoccupations of the nuns in the story were brought to light. Holy fools positioned themselves at the margins of church—outside enough to challenge the church to greater authenticity and humility while remaining faithful to the church. Likewise, the Rheinland nuns' playing positioned them on the borders of church, offering more female-centered practices of Christian formation. In both cases, these medieval Christians were leaning into a new creation in which women, the foolish, and others on the margins were taking their rightful place, while challenging to some degree the ecclesial and wider culture in which they lived.

---

89. Moltmann, *Theology of Play*, 12–13.

INSIGHTS FROM HISTORIC CASES OF REVELATORY EXPERIENCING

The lived experiences of Rheinland nuns, holy fools, and perhaps even those who played along with holy fools provide new insights for a developing theory of facilitating revelatory experiences. This historical perspective speaks critically to Winnicott and theological reflection on playing, in some cases filling in gaps where these fail to add understanding of revelatory experiences.

The playing of medieval saints builds on Winnicott's notion of cultural experience as transitional phenomena in ways that go beyond his clinical work. As a psychoanalyst, he is primarily interested in how cultural experience, including religion, can assist in the maturation of human beings by allowing them to live creatively. One could say that playing with devotional dolls exemplifies Winnicott's theory in that the ecclesial culture of the convent invited playing that fostered spiritual and psychic maturity. However, holy foolery brings complexity to Winnicott. Fools for Christ were playing in the midst of church culture that tolerated ecclesial power and wealth, yet this same culture permitted holy foolery to help liberate the faithful from this same captivity. While Winnicott is aware of the ways in which cultural experience can foster or hinder the maturation of the human person, he is not a social theorist and does not develop the implications of his theory for leadership or the formation of communities. However, the case of holy fools suggests how playing might creatively transform and strengthen groups of people. The fools were playing from an ethic of commitment to the wellbeing and liberation of fellow Christians. In some ways, this extends Winnicott's ideas by suggesting how, with the help of leadership, people can care for one another in ways that further both individuals as well as the group. Together the leaders and the group contribute to social change by creating what is countercultural—that is, a culture of being in relationship with one another in ways that lean into God's new creation.

The notion of creating change within individuals and culture by playing takes Moltmann in new directions as well. In light of holy foolery, being-with/and-for-others means more than being joyous with others in the midst of suffering. Some Western Catholic fools practiced child-like joy, but other fools were with/for the faithful in their ugliness as well. The scorn, humiliation, and arrogance that some fools evoked were authentic and spontaneous. These were not the emotions that Moltmann had in mind when he wrote of playing. However, for love's sake, the holy fools practiced being-with/and-for-others in places where the goodness of Christ was most absent. Moltmann had it right when he was reflecting on the need for "counter-environments" and being-with/for-others, but he was not able to write about what it looked like in practice, which is more emotionally messy than he realized.

Playing for love's sake provokes a wide range of emotions that makes revelatory experiencing powerful and varied. While the nuns played with quiet, joyful tenderness as they nurtured the Christ-child, holy fools played with fierce loving. These practices suggest a range of what human beings come to know in revelatory experiencing. Reflecting on nuns playing with devotional dolls, one can imagine that what one comes to know in joyful playing might be easily embraced. One might relish the experience. This would match Moltmann's understanding of playing as the celebration of life after Easter. However, the playing of holy fools suggests that playing can also bring the faithful to experience what they would rather not know—what they would rather keep hidden from consciousness or what has been "crucified" and buried. However, as holy foolery suggests, playing involves a "raising" of what has been buried so that it might be redeemed and transformed by Spirit. This is a less saccharine view of playing as Easter but perhaps more accurately attests to the liberative potential of playing that Moltmann himself had in mind.

Notions of where revelatory experiencing happens in religious education are kept expansive by the cases of nuns and fools. While playing with devotional dolls took place within convent walls in moments of quiet contemplation, holy foolery was enacted on the streets in everyday life. Many religious educators practice educational ministry beyond ecclesial structures, but it is perhaps less easy to imagine how revelatory experiencing might happen anywhere and everywhere, especially in contexts that are less familiar and quite diverse. The final chapter addresses this further.

Finally, the revelatory experiencing of medieval saints sheds new light on taken-for-granted assumptions about seeking spiritual knowledge. The truth of one's life cannot be sought directly by reason and logical deduction alone, but indirectly by "losing it" in playing with it. By becoming lost in the upside-down, surprising world of play for the sake of faith, it is possible to entertain what seems impossible: The baby Jesus is alive, crying for care. The savior can be found in the form of the fool on the street. A father turns against his son, a mother against her daughter. In playing, the faithful begin to grasp a divine wisdom that often runs counter to what human beings want or ostensibly need to believe. Lost in play, the faithful try on the radicalness of the life Jesus describes when he says that those who lose their life for his sake will find it.[90] Losing oneself for Christ's sake could also point to the necessity of playing at/in the new creation to grasp its paradoxes.

In becoming lost in play—holding the baby Jesus or becoming the fool—the faithful find and/or are found by Spirit. This adds a new twist to the hide-and-seek of Christian living. Humans have a tendency to hide from Spirit and self out of self-protection. However, if the faithful seek spiritual truth, sometimes they cannot seek it directly by sheer will or reason alone. Rather, they must also gain wisdom by losing themselves to playing at/in God's new creation, trusting they will find Spirit or Spirit will find them. Almost invariably, human beings are surprised to find or be found by Spirit. The paradox of losing oneself in playing is that it is both passive and active. One cannot make oneself feel lost in play. Trying too hard is not conducive to losing oneself. However, playing at/in the new creation is not a matter of waiting passively for Spirit to reveal itself either. The lesson of nuns and fools is that through traditions, practices, and ecclesial culture, communities create diverse containers for seeking and finding what is spiritually real.

From discussions of Winnicott, Moltmann's theology of play, other theological reflections on playing, and the historical examples of nuns and fools, some insights can be brought forward for building a theory of facilitating revelatory experiencing. First, playing allows learners to engage reality so that they can seek and find indirectly the grace-filled knowing they most need not only with the people around them but with Spirit. In doing so, they experience being lost and found or finding, which frees people for faith and abundance in relation to God and one another. Second, playing that invites revelatory experiencing involves love. Whether tender or fierce, maternal/paternal or childlike, human or divine, playing involves love that is authentic and life-giving, capable of surprising even hearts of stone. Third, playing that enables learners to live what is revelatory emerges from and responds to their needs, situated in a time and context. These insights form a base for further exploring the grounds for playing—or what helps playing to unfold.

90. Matthew 10:34–39.

chapter 5

PLAYING AESTHETICALLY: RETHINKING OUR GROUNDS FOR PLAYING

Grounds for playing is an important metaphor in multiple senses. *First*, it calls attention to the theoretical foundations of understanding playing. In this sense, psychoanalytic, theological, as well as historical perspectives ground playing in theory and context. The work has been to theorize in an interdisciplinary way what religious educators and learners create in the midst of revelatory experiencing. *Second*, grounds for playing bring to mind possible warrants—why humans of all ages play and why playing in/ at God's new creation is part of Christian life. *Third*, the notion of grounds for playing also connotes that playing happens in a space with real bodies, as the word *playground* suggests.[1] While there are many spaces for playing, faith communities and their many contexts of religious education are places for believers to play. Before the Protestant Reformation, there were no pews in the sanctuary because the faithful were meant to wander and wonder, to engage icons, and to light candles during worship.[2] The sanctuary space allowed and encouraged the faithful to play freely, to explore a world of possibilities. The notion of grounds for playing is vital in a *fourth* sense: while the theoretical grounds for playing are fertile, they also need rethinking or re-tilling as the image suggests. With its focus on space and the body, the third sense of grounds for playing churns the theoretical foundations and justifications for playing, enacting the fourth sense of grounds for playing, which is disturbing and enriching the theoretical grounds for playing and the implications for practice.

1. Roebben, "Playground for Transcendence," 332–47.
2. Chirovsky, "Anathema 'Sit,'" 167, 171.

In what follows, a contemporary example of liturgical art calls attention to the physical, psychic, cultural, and ecclesial spaces for Christians playing.[3] Liturgy itself can be understood as a practice that invites playing in/at God's new creation, though not everyone experiences worshipping as playing or thinks of it in these terms. The Puritans, who were wary of human weakness and ungodly behavior, strictly forbade levity on the Sabbath, including dancing or mirthful music in liturgy.[4] However, a narrow view of playing as entertainment or frivolity misses a vital way of understanding how we are formed by liturgy. "The play of liturgy and its power to shape Christian life is . . . future-oriented in hope, and future-present in foretaste."[5] Across liturgical seasons, hymns remind the faithful of what God promises, while the Eucharistic feast foreshadows the coming "heavenly banquet."[6] Of course, practicing liturgy has purposes and it invites experiences other than playing, but playing is among them. Reminiscent of a game, liturgy proceeds by way of forms and rules that have been passed on through Christian traditions. Liturgy teaches not by transmitting a set of concepts,[7] but by way of learning through experience and repeated practice. One who experiences playing in liturgy might perceive it as "a universe brimming with fruitful spiritual life, and [allow] the soul to wander about in it at will and to develop itself there."[8] Through playing, a person can yield to a liturgical universe, become steeped in it, and explore its possibilities.

Multiple perspectives on playing (psychoanalytic, theological, and historical) have brought more fully into view profound awakenings that religious educators facilitate but may have not symbolized or considered methodically. I have called this *revelatory experiencing* as a shorthand that connotes its importance for religious education. No single perspective on playing has been adequate to illumine what is being created in revelatory experiencing. Even taken together, what has been presented thus far is an incomplete account. What follows is a case of liturgical art that calls for rethinking the grounds for playing. A contemporary example from a Japanese American church brings to light aesthetic features of playing that psychoanalytic, theological, and historical perspectives on playing neglect.

3. Guardini, *Spirit of the Liturgy*, 66; Flanagan, "Liturgy as Play," 345–72.

4. Saliers, "Liturgy as Holy Play," 42.

5. Ibid.

6. Ibid.

7. Guardini, *Spirit of the Liturgy*, 66.

8. Ibid.

The example gives rise to a fourth analytic perspective on playing, which I call *local practical theological aesthetics*.

Associating aesthetics with playing is hardly new. Friedrich von Schiller wrote about "aesthetical play" in 1794, displaying remarkable forward thinking.[9] He references nature to illustrate how imagination, which he understands as a natural, wild, and abundant energy, makes the leap into aesthetical play as it finds form and creates beauty.[10] In finding an object to call beautiful, a person's imagining gives way to form, endowing the object with personality, creating it as it were.[11] Taking the association of aesthetics with play even further, Hans-Georg Gadamer goes so far as to argue that art *is* play, meaning play is "the mode of being of the work of art itself."[12] He is primarily interested in play as a means of describing what art is, rather than understanding play as something a person does. In contrast, when I refer to "playing aesthetically," I sometimes mean playing with/through art, where art is a medium for playing. However, playing aesthetically is not limited to art since all playing has aesthetic dimensions. In this sense, "playing aesthetically" refers to the sensual, imagistic, and affective dimensions of playing.

CREATING A PRETEND GARDEN AT A JAPANESE AMERICAN CHURCH

In California, the Sacramento Japanese United Methodist Church (SJUMC) experienced *The Garden Series*, a liturgical art installation based on the imagery of the changing seasons. This church has been playing aesthetically for over twenty-five years, as Naomi Takahashi Goto (my mother) has enhanced the church's worship with visual art.[13] The church was founded by Japanese immigrants; their fourth—and in some cases fifth generation— descendants now compose the church. The church has been affectionately called the "Garden Church" because of the "Japanese-style"[14] memorial garden at the heart of the church grounds (see fig. 1.0).

9. Schiller, "Letters."
10. Ibid.
11. Ibid., 308.
12. Gadamer, *Truth and Method*, 108–10.
13. Goto, "Pretending," 440–55.
14. Brown, *Japanese-Style Gardens*.

**Figure 1: Issei Memorial Garden, Sacramento Japanese United Methodist Church;
Photo courtesy of the author.**

My analysis of *The Garden Series* is part of larger ethnographic study of art, playing, and performance at SJUMC.[15] The research method involved conducting twenty-six interviews and engaging in participant observation over a period of two years. Eight of the interviews were related to *The Garden Series*. I also analyzed photographs and video recordings documenting the installation.

SJUMC was recovering from a divisive conflict over church property, finances, and church leadership. Working with pastor Motoe Yamada Foor (SJUMC pastor, 2009 to present), the artist created *The Garden Series* to help the congregation imagine a new future through playing. While it was the pastor who came up with the metaphor of the garden, it was my mother's role to translate the concept into art. She engaged children and adults in creating an indoor garden (made from wood, fabric, and paper) during worship over four weeks. The series visually mimicked the changing seasons to reflect the themes of forgiveness, communal growth, and transformation, while the pastor preached on these key themes.

---

15. Goto, "Artistic Play"; Goto, "Issei Garden."

The series gave the congregation playful opportunities to see their situation afresh. First, this was achieved by the art inviting creative participation. A focal point of the series was a free-standing, life-sized tree that needed the congregation's participation to "grow" from barren ("Winter," week one; see fig. 2.1), to sprouting leaves ("Spring," week two; see fig. 2.2 and fig. 2.3), to bearing fruit ("Summer/Fall," week three; see fig. 2.4), to being in a garden in full bloom ("God's New Creation," week four; see fig. 2.5). In the second week, members of the congregation were given leaves upon which to write what they were willing to do to participate in change at the church. During the worship service, the leaves were glued on the tree, transforming the barren tree to a greening one. In the third week, children were given bright red *origami* "fruit" to hang on the tree, as a sign of the congregation's willingness to "bear fruit." With wonder and surprise, members of the congregation witnessed what they had made together. Other elements were added between Sundays so that when the congregation arrived, they could discover new elements that had "grown" on the walls of the sanctuary. Each week, church members were eager to return and see how the garden had "bloomed."

Figure 2.1: "Winter," *The Garden Series*, by Naomi Takahashi Goto, Sacramento Japanese United Methodist Church; Photo courtesy of the artist.

Figure 2.2: "Spring," (Altar view) *The Garden Series*, by Naomi Takahashi Goto, Sacramento Japanese United Methodist Church; Photo courtesy of the artist.

Figure 2.3: "Spring," (Left view of sanctuary) *The Garden Series*, by Naomi Takahashi Goto, Sacramento Japanese United Methodist Church; Photo courtesy of the artist.

Figure 2.4: "Summer/Fall," *The Garden Series*, by Naomi Takahashi Goto, Sacramento Japanese United Methodist Church; Photo courtesy of the artist.

Figure 2.5: "God's New Creation," *The Garden Series*, by Naomi Takahashi Goto, Sacramento Japanese United Methodist Church; Photo courtesy of the artist.

A PSYCHOANALYTIC PERSPECTIVE

Two psychoanalytic concepts help to reveal how *The Garden Series* addressed tension within the congregation by facilitating creative, liberative ways of relating to and being with one another. The first is Winnicott's notion of the "good enough mother," and the second is Paul Pruyser's notion of "tutoring the imagination." Both have implications for pedagogies of playing.

Winnicott observed that good enough mothers (or parents) are key in helping their babies mature by providing conditions that facilitate their spontaneity and creativity. In this conducive environment, baby's needs are met by mother's matching, as she provides just enough of her presence and attention so that baby feels seen and held, though not held too tightly or supervised zealously. A home that is rigid, authoritarian, or controlling results in the child shutting down into compliant, submissive behavior. Overtaken by false self, true self is unable to express creativity and experience the feeling of aliveness. However, a good enough mother helps to establish a deep enough sense of trust and safety so that the child is able to play freely. In the pairing of mother and child, baby makes tentative gestures of creativity, testing to see how they will be received. A baby bangs a cup and a spoon together with delight and looks to mother for her reaction. The mother's role is to "be the environment" that embraces the child's spontaneous creativity with tolerance and understanding.[16] Mother and baby must "live an experience together" (in the words of Winnicott) in order for baby to mature.[17] Paradoxically, "living an experience together serves to separate the mother and infant (to bring them 'into relation with each other' as separate entities, from the infant's perspective)."[18]

In calling a mother "good enough," Winnicott was attempting to describe the ordinary gifts of a mother who naturally adapts to baby's needs out of her devotion to the child.[19] As a pediatrician, his theories were based on observing the practices and interactions of mothers and babies. His intention was not to impose theory onto practice, but rather to allow practice to inspire his theory. Ordinary good mothers are already good enough as they are.[20]

---

16. Winnicott, *Maturational Processes*, 76.

17. Winnicott, *Paediatrics*, 152.

18. Ogden, "Reading Winnicott," 315.

19. Winnicott, *Paediatrics*, 245.

20. Ibid.

This notion of "good enough" has implications for claiming gifts for the ministry of teaching. Although Jesus' disciples were flawed people, they too were "good enough" to do great deeds for the sake of God's new creation.[21] Likewise, despite their shortcomings, religious educators can be "good enough" to participate in and to facilitate transformation. Good enough educators have much practical wisdom and good instincts about how to nurture people into deeper faith. Thanks in part to this work, churches and other faith communities are also good enough at being the facilitative environments that the faithful need for maturing into faith.

In *The Garden Series*, the church leaders served as good enough mothers, doing what Winnicott says is helpful in raising a child, which is to impart a sense of baby's own creativity. (When I refer to the good enough mother, I mean *mother* in the wider sense of mother-figure, which can include men.) At first, a mother fosters a child's sense of creativity by attentively providing the breast whenever baby needs it, allowing baby to sense his/her power to summon (seemingly out of nowhere) what is imagined. In the church case, helping people to experience their creativity anew was helpful in imagining a new future—in a sense, progressing to a new developmental stage. In childhood, the mother plays with the child, receiving baby's spontaneous gestures with great appreciation. A good enough mother intuitively senses how to go along with a child's playing, enhancing it by pretending with the child and contributing to the playing. Likewise in *The Garden Series*, good enough educators not only left playthings "lying around" (as Winnicott says) to be taken up by church members (e.g., the tree, the leaves, and the fruit).[22] In addition, leaders responded to what the faithful created both in the sermons and in between Sundays, much like a mother would respond to what baby has created. The excitement of playing together came in "living an experience," in which people did not simply exist in the same space, but "respond[ed] to one another's separate acts" in the living of an experience.[23] Church members delighted in what they made in collaboration with one another.

The analogy of the good enough mother works in two ways—first from the perspective of institutions and then from that of individuals. From an ecclesial point of view, this Japanese American church follows a long

21. For reflection on Simon Peter as a flawed but good enough disciple, see Perkins, "Flawed Disciple," 12–23.

22. Winnicott, *Maturational Processes*, 99.

23. Ogden, "Reading Winnicott," 315.

tradition of churches doing what a good enough mother does in facilitating playing, which is to "be" a supportive environment. In this sense, the Roman Catholic and Orthodox churches were functioning as a good enough mother to the holy fools and the Rheinland nuns. The notion of "mother church" has meaning in both traditions. Ecclesial structures and traditions provided enough freedom and a sense of holding to develop these radical practices. In the case of holy fools, the mother church even tolerated the critique of holy fools, which scorned the power and pretentiousness of church hierarchy.[24] At the same time, the holy fools were still embraced as part of the church in all their glorious creativity and seemingly bizarre behavior. This is not unlike the way in which mothers allow their toddlers to play freely, albeit under a watchful eye. Some might feel that the image of the church as a parent is condescending, but it is important to remember that all Christians constitute "the church."

The art installation was offered in an ecclesial context, so one could indeed refer to the role of "mother church," but it was also an individual mother who created it out of love for her church family. Good enough religious educators abound. They anticipate the revelatory experiencing that might be needed in the moment, though it cannot be controlled or predicted entirely. Even then, it is not only religious educators serving as mothers, but also Christians and others who facilitate playing with one another. In most contexts of religious education, teachers are lay people who take turns leading.

Dual senses of good enough mothering (institutional and individual) come together as church serves as a basis for leaders facilitating life-giving relationships with one another and the church being a place where playing is practiced. Under the leadership of religious educators, the church provides the time, space, practices, media, and supervision for playing in/ at the God's new creation.[25] Gary Barbaree (SJUMC pastor from 1985–91) describes the church as a sandbox where designated leaders keep close watch over how playing unfolds so that no one gets hurt while people play with scary issues, including issues of life, death, transformation, justice, and mercy. According to Barbaree, the sacramental utensils are "toys" for Christians to play and practice with. Just as a little boy learns with a toy hammer how to use a real one safely, so too "the bread that we eat is a toy

24. Ivanov, *Holy Fools*, 404.

25. Rich, "Grace and Imagination," 218; Acklin, "Adult Maturational Processes," 198–206.

body. The cup that we drink is toy blood. And what we hope . . . is when the time comes that we deal with real flesh and blood during the week, we've had some experience with that already."[26] The measures, structures, and materials that churches provide help to establish trust with believers so that they feel that it is safe enough to enter the healthy illusions being offered, which are sacred to the community.

The Garden Series is illumined by a second concept, Paul Pruyser's notion of "tutoring the imagination."[27] As a psychologist with an interest in religion, Pruyser was influenced by Winnicott's ideas. Pruyser argues that healthy adults are trained in entering healthy illusions through symbols, narratives, and objects that create a vivid, coherent world—a religious world being one of them.[28] People enjoy becoming increasingly skilled at entering into what Pruyser calls an "illusionistic world."[29] Much of education (in this case religious education) is geared toward teaching people how to participate in the healthy illusions appropriate to a context.[30] Developing this "cultural game" with others is fulfilling and meaningful as believers' internal, felt sense of reality becomes expressed externally and shared symbolically.[31] Through the illusion of religion, one "begins to see a wider horizon of possibilities,"[32] in this case, in Christ. One could argue that *The Garden Series* enlisted church members to create a colorful, fictive world that invited them to play in/at God's new creation.

Pruyser locates the illusionistic world between what he calls the "autistic" and "realistic" worlds of perception, building on Winnicott's notions of the intermediate space between subjectivity and objectivity. Pruyser warns that, left alone, a person can allow imagination to stray toward one sphere or another, neither of which fosters the healthy illusions involved in playing.[33] One possibility—indeed, one risk or danger—is to permit one's imagination to drift toward "autistic thinking," allowing imagination to become distorted or lost in private fantasy, hallucinations, or narcissism.[34]

26. Gary Barbaree, interview with the author, April 3, 2008.

27. Pruyser, *Play of the Imagination.*

28. Pruyser, "Lessons from Art Theory," 7–8.

29. Pruyser, *Play of the Imagination*, 63.

30. Ibid., 70.

31. Pruyser, "Lessons from Art Theory," 11.

32. Ibid.

33. Pruyser, *Play of the Imagination*, 64–65.

34. Ibid., 65.

Another is to allow one's imagination to be hampered by "realistic thinking."[35] When a person is absorbed in realistic thinking, ideas and propositions can become reified over and against mystery.[36] Both of these practices detract from playing and foreclose its possibilities.

Pruyser's notion of tutoring the imagination is a helpful way to think about the challenges of forming and guiding imagination for the sake of faith. On one hand, religious educators should be vigilant of imagination trapped in autistic thinking. Imagination can be led intentionally or unintentionally into delusion or destructive fantasies. To some extent, Christian traditions have been right to be wary of imagination, especially as it can be manipulated to unholy ends.[37] For religious educators, this raises questions about how to guide, limit, and anticipate imagination, which is not fully predictable. On the other hand, embracing an opposite approach—realistic thinking instead of autistic thinking—also creates problems but in reverse, imposing too much control. It can be reassuring to have concrete beliefs and a set of rules by which to live that one deeply believes is godly. For some Christians, being sure that one is conforming to God's will and Christian doctrine is essential to faith. However, realistic thinking in practicing faith has its limitations, as does any single approach to theology. In this "realistic" way of thinking, one might assume that religious propositions can be proven by seemingly self-evident, hard "facts," leaving little room for entertaining possibilities for imagination or subjective interpretation.[38] When teaching veers too strongly toward the transfer of information, it is easy to stray into a "realistic" mindset in teaching. Even well intended educators can override the unfolding poetry of the moment or overlook spontaneous opportunities to create in favor of conforming to "the plan" and conveying "the facts."

Achieving the happy middle in teaching is not easy but key for revelatory experiencing. Each instance of religious education is unique, involving different learners and processes. Learners themselves have different capacities and propensities for engaging in autistic and realistic thinking, as do the educators themselves and the communities of which they are part. The task is then to consider, moment by moment, what is needed to guide

35. Ibid., 64–65.

36. Ibid., 176.

37. For more on imagination in Christian tradition, see Kearney, *Wake of Imagination*, 40.

38. Pruyser, *Play of the Imagination*, 177.

imagination toward illusionistic thinking given all these variables, adapting to the learners and the situation as it is unfolding.

In addressing tension at SJUMC, leaders guided congregants' imagining and relating to one another through *The Garden Series*. Through the participatory nature of the art, educators accompanied members of the congregation as the learning unfolded, discouraging either autistic or realistic thinking along the way. Because the pretend garden explicitly drew on imagery of the living garden outside, the artist provided less opportunity for completely free association or autistic thinking. The preacher also guided imagination through theological reflection on the changing art images. In addition, *The Garden Series* offered new visual poetry each week, continually inviting interpretation and subverting realistic thinking. For example, there was fabric evocatively draped on the walls, which suggested trees (to my eye) but without defining or imposing meaning. In the Winter week, brown "trees" lined the walls close to the front of the sanctuary. In the Spring week, green "trees" were added to the walls toward the back of the sanctuary. Finally in Spring/Summer weeks, red "trees" appeared, completing the progression. Members of the congregation were free to interpret what these images were and what they meant. The freedom to interpret and the challenge of interpreting contributed to the power and delight of playing.

A THEOLOGICAL PERSPECTIVE

In *Theology of Play*, Moltmann argues that Christians should become "congregations of the liberated," as they practice being-with/for-others.[39] He envisions Christians being in relationship with the oppressed and marginalized so that all might experience the joy of liberation. In my revision of Moltmann's work, I suggested that Christians are to embody hope through empathic, life-giving relationships, which can accommodate a wide range of emotional states and be experienced in a variety of situations, including those not associated with common understandings of playing.

The story of the sinful woman drawn to Jesus while he is at the house of Simon the Pharisee is a helpful text to fill out Moltmann's argument. The woman washes Jesus' feet with her tears, dries them with her hair, and dresses them with ointment.[40] By my account, her actions can be under-

39. Moltmann, *Theology of Play*, 71.

40. Luke 7:36–50.

stood as playing. She pretends that her tears are bathing water and acts "as if" her hair were a towel. Her earnest tears suggest she is acting spontaneously and authentically. The felt rightness of what she does is evident in the outpouring of her devotion. Her behavior does not conform to what is expected of her, which is to stay away from Jesus and the home of a Pharisee. She is able to play in Jesus' presence because he has created a space that makes it safe enough to defy social norms. (In a Winnicottian sense, Jesus provides a *facilitating environment* or *holding environment*.) He nurtures, affirms, and appreciates the heartfelt gestures of the sinful woman. He does not question what she is doing, but rather recognizes what a beautiful thing she has done. By letting her wash his feet with her tears and allowing her to dry them with her hair, he participates with her in playing. He does not simply acknowledge what she has done, he plays with her, living an experience. The pairing allows the woman to grow in relationship to Christ. Interestingly, Simon represents an all-too-familiar, legalistic, or controlling figure who passes judgment on the woman's behavior. As the story goes, Jesus argues for a posture of empathy, attunement, and participation with the woman, much like a human mother (or good enough church) would do.

This text provides vision for how churches might lovingly be-with/ for-others, as Jesus facilitated the sinful woman's playing. They were both *playing for love's sake.* Although Moltmann does not give examples of what "congregations of the liberated" might look like, *The Garden Series* stirs the imagination of a congregation that follows Jesus' example, perhaps in the way that Moltmann could appreciate. In the story, Jesus does not dictate a solution to the woman's problems. He does not appear to be teaching anything directly. His role is to create a space in which she can create what she needs, enabled by his loving presence and his willingness to hold one who has been shunned. He extends hospitality to her, which was meaningful to her as a woman on the margins of society. Likewise, in the church example, the artist created a space in which members of the church, on all sides of the conflict, could come together and create—possibly what they needed. There was no distinguishing who was right and who was wrong. There was no judgment. No Simons were allowed to derail the playing. Church members were invited as fellow brothers and sisters in Christ to set aside their differences, at least while playing, to create with one another something beautiful and potentially transformative. They could re-experience themselves as children of God in light of what they made.

When Moltmann writes of being-with/for others in playing, he has in mind the strangers outside of one's community, which is important but incomplete. Being in solidarity with the marginalized, the poor, and the oppressed will always be a Christian imperative. However, *The Garden Series* suggests that in order to lean into God's new creation, one must also bring into relationship those *within* the community who have been estranged. Moltmann uses the language of playing to express his vision that churches be "testing grounds" for God's new creation.[41] Though he does not give details about what this might look like, *The Garden Series* provides a glimpse of one congregation.

While psychoanalytic perspectives help to explain how human culture forms people into the healthy illusions of faith, one might prefer to think of playing as occasions for Spirit to "practice in us."[42] Playing creates openings for Spirit so that God is tutoring us for more abundant living. Spirit uses human imagination (and other gifts) to its own ends of liberation and sanctification.[43] On its own, imagination might stray into autistic or realistic worlds, but Spirit directs imagination so that it might be formed for love's sake. In guiding imagination, Spirit reveals itself and the faithful are "found" by Spirit. In the church example, *The Garden Series* created a space in which church members could come out of "hiding" or the sense of wounding that some may have experienced in the conflict.

A HISTORICAL PERSPECTIVE

Historical perspectives on *The Garden Series* illumine the church's playing in a larger context. *The Garden Series* draws on the imagery of the Issei Memorial Garden, located in the heart of the church grounds. This 1,556 square-foot plot is beautifully landscaped with Japanese maple, pine, and cherry trees, azalea, camellia, granite rock, and river stones. It allows for the serene contemplation and remembrance of the first generation (*issei*) pioneers of the church and others who have passed on. As Japanese immigrants to the United States before World War II, the *issei* generation suffered economic hardship, racism, and incarceration with their families in wartime relocation camps. The Issei Garden honors their perseverance, sacrifices, and faith.

41. Moltmann, *Theology of Play*, 70.
42. Stubbs, "Practices," 20.
43. McIntyre, *Shape of Pneumatology*, 271.

The garden was constructed by church members and dedicated in 1972, when the church was newly merged, but it fell into decline in the 1990s due to lack of expertise. Since 2002, volunteers, called "Garden Angels," most of whom are men, have revitalized the garden by using traditional Japanese pruning techniques done by hand, which are time and labor intensive.[44] The images and stories of the construction, revitalization, and care of the Issei Garden are sacred to the community. The link between the Issei Garden and the toy garden was made with a recounting of the history of the Issei Garden and Garden Angels giving testimonies of faith during *The Garden Series.* Men from the Garden Angels spoke publicly for the first time about why they dedicate themselves to beautifying the garden and the church's landscaping. This is a community whose older generation of Japanese American men prefers to live their faith than talk about it.[45] They would rather (in the words of Paul) "be doers of the word and not merely hearers who deceive themselves."[46] Addressing their faith, the Garden Angels who spoke enacted a new way of being together (a new creation). The conflict at the church was so critical that it summoned these men to "do something," allowing themselves to be seen and heard as never before.

Linking *The Garden Series* explicitly and artistically to the Issei Garden signaled the present as a pivotal time to move forward by linking it with the construction of the Issei Garden, which was a turning point in the church's history. The Issei Garden was built as two Japanese American congregations were coming together and finding strength in their unity.[47] Furthermore, *The Garden Series* evoked the memory of the *issei* generation's courageous spirit—their determination to move forward even in the most difficult of circumstances.

INSIGHTS FROM AN AESTHETIC CASE OF REVELATORY EXPERIENCING

While psychoanalytic, theological, and historical perspectives are critically needed, *The Garden Series* presents its own wisdom about the *aesthetic* dimensions of revelatory experiences. As I argue in the next section, these insights are significant for rethinking the grounds for playing.

44. Goto, "Issei Garden," 76–97.

45. Jonathan Sakakibara, interview with the author, March 31, 2009.

46. James 1:22 quoted in Miyahara, "Dear Ben."

47. Goto, "Issei Garden."

First, *The Garden Series* suggests that the physical space of playing can be vital for engaging learners in revelatory experiencing. The toy tree, the fabric "woods," and other visual motifs altered the feel, the colors, and the focus of the space. While a large cross and the altar normally dominate the chancel, *The Garden Series* shifted the gaze to the pretend tree, located near the pulpit. What was indoors was made to look like the outdoors, and what was outside was brought inside, in a playful reversal of indoor and outdoor, liturgical and everyday spaces, as well as building and garden. All of these spatial alterations and re-imagined symbols of spaces decentered the sanctuary, "making the familiar seem strange *in order to enhance [the] perception of the familiar.*"[48] Historically, in a church building the narthex indicates passage from outer to inner—a transition to a holy space, which is to be regarded differently from what is outside the sanctuary. Much of the historic meaning of church architecture is lost on many church members. However, *The Garden Series* helped the faithful to experience anew the transitions between profane and sacred worlds, with corresponding shifts between realistic and illusionistic thinking.

The Garden Series awakened creativity and the senses, which is a second aesthetic dimension of revelatory experiencing. The installation guided church members to be creative in being with each other, making something never before seen. Furthermore, the series activated a fuller range of the senses than what the space usually demands on a Sunday. The garden sanctuary altered a person's kinesthetic and spatial sense. Bodies were invited to sense, move, and act in ways new to SJUMC's liturgy, including participating in and making visual art over the course of a worship service. Transformation was not simply discussed in the abstract or as a proposition; it was contemplated creatively, spatially, and aesthetically as church members witnessed what transformation might look like in symbolic form or what it might feel like to act in new ways. One could draw parallels from *The Garden Series* to the ways in which creativity and the senses were summoned and formed in caring for the *Puppen*. The nuns touched, dressed, as well as gazed at the dolls in order to enter into creative relationship with them. An important difference is that *The Garden Series* was a limited engagement, which perhaps might have allowed some members of the congregation to play more readily, and be more creative and open to new sense experiences. People knew that the sanctuary space and appearance would revert to normal once the series was over.

48. Smith, *Imagining Religion*, xiii.

Third, the aesthetic appeal of the sanctuary garden summoned affective responses that contributed to possible revelatory experiencing. Though there was likely a range of emotional responses to the art, interviews suggest that some church members were swept up in the wonder, surprise, and the goodness of a new creation. These feelings were vital to rejuvenating the congregation and inspiring a willingness to reinvest in the church and one another. These affective responses might have been more difficult to facilitate without playing aesthetically, yet they were vital to promoting what needed to be experienced. Similarly, the holy fools were provoking affective responses that were key to revelatory experiencing of a different kind. Here too, people in medieval everyday life were moved by aesthetic situations orchestrated by fools for Christ.

All three of these aesthetic dimensions of revelatory experiencing (space, creativity and the senses, as well as affective responses) foster a fourth—a sense of bonding between participants, tied to a specific time and context. When people share bodily, aesthetic experiences, they enter into something that others could not know or fully understand because they were not there. One could describe *The Garden Series*, but words do not capture what was lived together. Moments of playing in *The Garden Series* could not be replicated because they addressed the needs of a particular moment in the life of the church. Playing is ephemeral, being both time and context sensitive, yet it connects participants to one another in the living of an experience. In the future, church members are likely to remember not so much the words that were said, but the sensual, creative, affective experience of making the sanctuary garden together.

Taking an aesthetic perspective helps to identify what is often taken for granted in revelatory experiencing. Traditionally, the focal point of communion is a common table that defines the space. The practice trains the imagination, creativity, and the senses in a sensual feast of memory, even as these three shape the meaning of the practice. Since the early church from at least Irenaeus on in the second century, the Eucharist has been understood as a "school of the senses."[49] The senses, especially taste, are heightened in the Eucharist, guiding the soul and the intellect, rather than the opposite.[50] Finally, the practice of communion is intended to provoke affective responses that form people in faith. The experience is meant to bind up the faithful in the moment of taking communion together. While

49. Gorringe, *Education of Desire*, 104.
50. Méndez, *Theology of Food*, 69.

leaders hope that partaking of the Lord's Supper will involve awakening to deep truths, the routineness of the practice—while essential and formative in many respects—can also make it difficult for the faithful to find new meaning in the familiar. Experiencing it afresh is more challenging than a one-time art installation, which has novelty as an advantage.

Churches and other contexts of religious education serve as key aesthetic spaces in which the faithful receive assistance to navigate the perils of being human in a shifting church and world. In *The Garden Series*, church members needed assistance in shifting out of conflict. In transitions such as these, playing aesthetically is key as sacred stories and rituals help participants to explore safely the mysteries of birth, death, and even tragedy. Within hallowed grounds for playing, the faithful are tutored and assisted in holding what feels too big to hold on one's own. One observes this in worship, which tutors the faithful to withstand what seems irreconcilable—the sublime "beauty" of life and the "terror" of that which threatens to engulf and destroy.[51] In the celebration of Holy Week, the faithful are tutored to stay present to the "beauty and terror" of being human, which is made meaningful in light of Christ.[52]

The Garden Series took advantage of the power of imitation or *mimesis*, which allows for the re-presenting and re-seeing of what is essential but perhaps hidden. Mimicry is a common way of playing in general and playing with/through art in particular. Dressing up in costumes or playing follow-the-leader are favorite children's games, but art also imitates life in illuminating respects. In this regard, Aristotle "claims that the joy we take in imitation is really the joy of recognition."[53] In imitation, the delight of recognition is in the revealing of "the real essence of a thing."[54] In mimicking the Issei Garden, the toy garden made present the essence of the Issei Garden. The story of the Issei Garden is one of transformation and recovery of what was almost lost. The Issei Garden could not reveal its own essence as readily as the toy garden. The imitation was freed from "contingent circumstances" in which the original is continually seen.[55] In other words, the toy garden allowed the Issei Garden to be seen afresh. This assisted the church members to imagine a brighter future, having seen the present

---

51. Saliers, "Beauty and Terror," 303–13.

52. Ibid.

53. Gadamer, *Relevance of the Beautiful*, 98.

54. Ibid., 99.

55. Ibid.

moment in light of their historic strengths. In the process of imitation, one recognizes oneself or in this case, the community recognizes itself.[56]

One can also ponder whether the people were mimicking the art or whether the art was mimicking the people. Paper dolls, which were tacked to the chancel wall, were scattered in the first week, but they slowly joined together over the course of the series, until they were seen holding hands in a circle by the end. By participating in the art, church members were mimicking the art (or vice versa), making real what the art was pointing to.[57] The Garden Angels spontaneously offered live plants and a *bonsai* tree to be added to the final Sunday of the Garden series, making the image of the new creation more real. More generally, building the pretend garden was a re-enactment of constructing the live garden outside. In any case, *The Garden Series* assisted church members in moving forward from conflict not only by seeing a new vision of themselves but by *enacting one aesthetically.*

RE-TILLING GROUNDS FOR PLAYING

Insights from *The Garden Series* suggest that while they are important, by themselves psychoanalytic, theological, and historical perspectives on playing provide too thin an account of what was created in revelatory experiencing. An aesthetic perspective is a necessary fourth lens. In all its aesthetic fullness, the revelatory experiencing of *The Garden Series* builds upon and in some cases unsettles the grounds upon which playing have been established thus far.

Playing with space in *The Garden Series* gives flesh to Pruyser's notion of tutoring imagination to help people enter an "illusionistic world." While his account is sensitive to enacting or adopting ways of being and doing that allow people to participate in healthy illusions, within his argument is an assumption that could be made more explicit. By the way we practice being in the world (e.g., through art, science, literature, religion), the body and the senses are inextricably involved in the tutoring of imagination. *The Garden Series* makes this clear as the art immerses church members in an altered space. The art helps them to feel visually and kinesthetically "as if" they were somewhere else, yet to rediscover the grounds for playing (as in

---

56. Ibid., 100.

57. The use of paper dolls in *The Garden Series* is reminiscent of the practice of Japanese ambassador dolls and American friendship dolls. See Museum of International Folk Art, "Miss Yamaguchi."

a playground) that were always there. *The Garden Series* refines Pruyser's notion of the "tutoring of imagination," by suggesting that it is at least partly through the body and the senses that imagination is formed.

Winnicott's theory about the mother-child dyad also has within its depths some important ideas about space, body, and aesthetic experience that might be further elaborated upon. The love experienced at infancy is expressed bodily by mother. "As Winnicott emphasizes, we depend on a woman's holding us in our body, handling our body as milk, as arms, as hands that wash and feed us, as eyes that look into our own, as ears that answer our communiqués with her voice and actions, as skin with her own distinct fragrance."[58] The very first ways that we register and know love are through the senses in the intimacy of being held and touched. Winnicott gives clues about the importance of this sensual holding that happens in the mother child dyad; however, to imagine how this happens communally, in the context of a particular culture, requires further thought. This primal way of registering through the senses being loved is essential not only to human maturation but to the growth of Christian faith.

The Garden Series addresses a key question of how members of Christ's body "imaginatively hold one another in being" in order to play for love's sake.[59] The installation uses aesthetics and familiar imagery from the Issei Garden to offer the opportunity for the congregation to feel held and to hold one another. The art serves as a kind of container that communicates aesthetically both interest in and care for the community's needs, registering to the senses a bodily being-with through participation with the art and one another. In a time of disunity, experiencing a heightened bodily sense of being with one another in new ways offered healing opportunities for church members. In general, "[r]eligion points to the safe environment provided by the God who holds us in being,"[60] even in the fragmentation of being human both as individuals and in community. Not only is there estrangement within human beings, for example a splitting of mind from body, there is the fracturing of Christ's body that needs to be healed. This too is part of leaning into God's new creation.

Winnicott is sensitive to the aesthetic dimensions of baby's first transitional objects, but others have extended his thinking more explicitly.[61] A

58. Ulanov, *Finding Space*, 44.

59. Ibid., 47.

60. Ibid., 49.

61. Rudnytsky, *Transitional Objects*.

blanket or teddy bear is chosen because its aesthetic qualities (its softness and warmth) match the feel of mother. The match is good enough for mother to be recreated and "found" in the substitute. Inspired by Winnicott and others, object relations aesthetics has built upon this notion of "finding fit" with objects that we seek and find and thereby create. (Sometimes we literally create as in the case of making art.) Christopher Bollas argues that adults engage in a lifelong search for "transformational objects" that create an "aesthetic moment" of "fitting with" an object as it evokes existential memory.[62] Building on the work of Winnicott, Bollas traces early experiences of transformational objects to interactions between mother and baby. However, in Bollas' work the significance of the mother is less as an object and more as a "process that is identified with cumulative internal and external transformations."[63] As people mature, Bollas argues the search for transformational objects never ends. Art is understood to be a source of transformational objects that help us to integrate the self.

Bollas' theory offers possible contributions for thinking about revelatory experiencing. To some degree, his notion of "finding fit" is helpful in illumining what individuals may have experienced in *The Garden Series*. One could argue that members of the congregation who were moved by the art "found fit" with the imagery because it was drawn from the community's history, culture, and collective imaginary, which the Issei Garden symbolizes. Bollas' theory would predict that the "rapport" that members of the congregation found with the art evoked "existential memory . . . conveyed not through visual or abstract thinking but through the affects of being."[64] This is one explanation of why encounters with art can feel "uncanny" or "referential," as if the art were speaking to the audience in particular.[65]

However, Bollas' perspective has its limitations. Because art is a solitary experience in Bollas' theory, he focuses primarily on what is happening within an individual. However, for understanding revelatory experiencing, focusing solely on internal, individual experience misses what is so helpful in Winnicott, who understands that the heart of playing is what is created between and among players. Furthermore, Bollas' theory diminishes the role of object destruction. However, as we have seen in the case of devotional dolls, object destruction is critical to the revision of understanding

62. Bollas, *Shadow*, 31–32.
63. Ibid., 14.
64. Ibid, 40–41.
65. Ibid.

of who others are and who we are in relation to them. It is only when an internal image, idea, or a symbol of someone falls away that there is an opportunity for it to be challenged, revised, and perhaps created more accurately. When *The Garden Series* was dismantled, church members were perhaps more able to see the church anew, including essential truths that had been there all along.

Bollas offers the intriguing notion that baby is first transformed by the mother's aesthetic (or her form), but this too seems problematic. He argues that mother transforms baby's periodic experiences of hunger, aloneness, and need by providing a comforting, aesthetic experience of her body—whether in nursing, holding, or in changing diapers.[66] In Bollas' thinking, this primary experience is repeated later in life as people continue to find transformational objects. However, his understanding of baby's earliest aesthetic experiences implies an assumption that mother is acting upon baby rather than the two "living an experience together" heightened by mutual aesthetic engagement. In Bollas' model, the mutuality of playing is less clear. It overlooks the fact that aesthetic dimensions of playing together can intensify the creativity and spontaneity of both mother and child.

While *The Garden Series* extends and challenges some of the psychoanalytic concepts we have discussed, it makes evident some of Moltmann's limitations, first in terms of practical theology and second in terms of speaking to the oppressed. To start with, *The Garden Series* challenges Moltmann's notion that because playing is spontaneous it cannot be planned or orchestrated. On some level, he is correct in that the creativity of playing cannot be fully predicted. It does emerge in the moment. However, *The Garden Series* (and the historic examples in the previous chapter) suggest that religious educators can provide *conditions that foster playing together*. In *The Garden Series*, aesthetic teaching creates the grounds for playing (in the spatial sense). The visual marking of the "playground" provided the impetus for and the structure for playing. Playing is neither merely a symbol for aesthetic experience and life-giving relationships nor is theology primarily an act of imagination, as Moltmann assumes in his writing about play. Playing and theology can be embodied, aesthetic practices. *The Garden Series* suggests that Christians can not only think about but also "do theology" aesthetically, which can contribute to revelatory experiencing.

The Garden Series challenges Moltmann's perspective in a second regard. He writes from his own context and situation, which is a

66. Ibid., 41–42.

German-speaking theologian who was profoundly shaped by being a prisoner of war during World War II, living as a refugee, and suffering the shame of belonging to an oppressor nation guilty of heinous war crimes.[67] When Moltmann writes of being-with/for-others, he writes primarily to urge Christians who have power and privilege to be in solidarity with the poor and the marginalized. However, *The Garden Series* addresses a different audience, namely the oppressed themselves. A Japanese American congregation such as the one in Sacramento is not excused from the responsibility of being with/for the powerless. And while this church is privileged in terms of class and education, members of the congregation live with a legacy of racism and marginalization, which has shaped communal memory, identity, and theology. The case challenges Moltmann with its own practical theological aesthetic approach to being-with/for-others. *The Garden Series* attests to the internal healing that needs to happen within congregations, regardless of race and sometimes because of racism. It might also be the case that playing together must also address both communal and individual healing, which Moltmann does not address in his *Theology of Play.*

Moltmann does not go far enough in addressing the stranger within oneself. To a large extent, a person is obligated to comply to social norms, images of the media, and to familial expectations in order to fit in. However, not being a stranger to others can mean becoming a stranger to oneself, coping with a diminished ability to express one's authenticity or spontaneity. Without befriending the stranger within, one's participation in God's new creation is also encumbered. However, as *The Garden Series* suggests, playing creates opportunities for expressing authenticity and/or spontaneity. As people are surprised by their own playing, by being and doing in more authentic ways, they might discover that they are able to exist more often without protective barriers. This has implications, not only for those healing from the effects of oppression, but also for those willing to heal themselves of racist ways of thinking, feeling, and doing. All of this is in addition to Moltmann's being-with/for-others who are outside the community.

67. Müller-Fahrenholz, *Kingdom and the Power*, 17.

PLAYING WITH RENDITIONS

All of the examples in this book, including *The Garden Series*, involve Christians playing by creating *renditions*, which is my own term. Renditions are creative, situated versions or interpretations of what someone perceives. An artist renders the image of an object, a scene, a feeling, or an idea so that it might be communicated and known to others. A rendition implies a doing and a making that re-presents what is held to be true in a slightly different or mediated form, which draws attention to certain aspects but not others. In *The Garden Series*, church members created a rendition of God's new creation. More generally, renditions are the primary means by which Christians play together. Ritualizing renders mysteries of life through performance, images, and symbols. Psalms and hymns are poetic renditions of the heart and the human spirit's longing for God as it is expressed in words and music. Prayers express who we think God is and who we are as people of God. Even a theological lecture is a philosophical rendition. Many practices of faith allow Christians to render the holy in ways that the faithful can grasp, be grasped by, let go of, and perhaps revisit.

From a theological point of view, a rendition of God's new creation is an opportunity for a learning community to play at/in what is envisioned. Renditions of God's new creation act as a bridge[68] between the reality of the present moment and the dream of love. Creating and experiencing in/through a rendition is the practice of negotiating the difference and distance between what is and what may be, the not yet and the already. This is how playing gives the faithful hope for transformation seen and unseen, as well as hope for what is promised. A bridge to God's new creation can be found in the playing of holy fools or playing with/through liturgical art. For those who are new to faith, playing at/in the new creation creates a first-time bridge. For longtime Christians, standing on the bridge in between the here-and-now and the not-yet is a moment of rest, of reassurance, of "having" a bit of the new creation for one's own for a time. Having a "foretaste of glory divine" gives hope and vision for the new creation, renewing Christians in faith.[69]

Every occasion for religious education is an opportunity to create a rendition of what we hold as theologically true, while practicing an

---

68. Milner, *Suppressed Madness*, 103; Rose, *Power of Form*, 195; Sabbadini, "Bridge of Space," 17–30.

69. Crosby, "Blessed Assurance."

embodiment of the Gospel in relating to one another. In teaching and learning, we create an experience that we live together, which is co-created as participants are able to contribute as true self. With every rendition, one has the opportunity to sense what is newly brought into being and to compare past versions in an ongoing process of creation and revision. Playing comes from a faith community deepening, recreating, and developing its renditions with the help of religious educators.

Renditions are "counter-environments" (to use Moltmann's words) that offer alternative futures, but the notion of renditions adds a key aesthetic perspective. Communal renditions that deepen faith call attention to the fact that they come from tradition, a repertoire if you will. Like artistic renditions, they are multiple, varied, and evolving. Renditions are repeated because they are meaningful to the community, sometimes held as sacred. The repetition of renditions allows them to be lived into over time. No two renditions are exactly alike—from community to community and time to time even in the same community. Within a faith community, renditions have continuity because they come from the same store of aesthetic, cultural, and theological resources. Religious educators know that no teaching session, no liturgy, and no project of spiritual formation is the same twice nor is it entirely unrelated from what has been taught before. Like a work of art, each rendition of playing for the sake of faith is unique, yet still rooted in the community's resources.

DEVELOPING LOCAL PRACTICAL THEOLOGICAL AESTHETICS

How a faith community renders what it holds to be true is accomplished aesthetically, which impacts how teaching is experienced in the body and how what is taught conveys meanings that go beyond words. Aesthetics performs a vital role in determining how a learner's body and imagination are "handled" in the space of religion,[70] including the spaces in which religious education happens. Religion emerges in the place between "'natural aesthetics' (those dealing with sensory perception and rooted in the body) and 'artificial aesthetics' (those dealing with the objects and arts in the world, along with their creation and reception)."[71] This in-between, liminal space is where natural and artificial aesthetics are in dialectical tension with

70. Plate, "Skin of Religion," 165.
71. Ibid., 167.

one another in that one's senses are engaged and mediated by forms (images, symbols) given by religious tradition. Natural and artificial aesthetics work together and in tension with one another to "move human hearts."[72] (In a Winnicottian sense, this liminal space can be understood in terms of transitional phenomena.) In the space in-between, "sense perception is a central point of mediation for the reception, creation, and reproduction of social-sacred space."[73] Aesthetics creates space in which the faithful might experience more fully (through the fullness of human being) the mysteries that religion would have them experience.

If a faith community knows itself well enough, people can render their hopes, ideas, intuitions, feelings, and images of God's new creation in meaningful, aesthetic ways in which they are most able to be expressive. The "local aesthetics" speaks of and to the community by appealing to people's particular sensual preferences, their context, and their way of being in the world. The Rheinland nuns needed dolls because dolls spoke particularly to them. The Japanese American church in Sacramento needed the aesthetics, culture, and narrative of the Issei Garden.[74] A Charismatic church needs to pray in tongues.

Local practical theological aesthetics (LPTA) is the sensibilities that guide a Christian community's unique "style"[75] of relating form and theological content. A community's aesthetic sensibilities are based on their experiences of being "taken in" by God's beauty, which combines the sublimity of God's transcendence with the groundedness of God's vulnerability in taking human form.[76] A community employs these sensibilities by way of LPTA.

Because practical theological aesthetics involves taking context into account, the addition of the word *local* is a modest contribution. However, in the wider field of theological aesthetics, scholars have often approached revelation and art with little regard to context.[77] Referring to *local* practical theological aesthetics is analogous to Robert Schreiter's calling attention to "local theologies," provoking a shift from thinking about theology in com-

---

72. García-Rivera, *Community of the Beautiful*, 9.

73. Ibid., 168.

74. Goto, "Pretending"; ibid., "Artistic Play."

75. Louw, "Creative Hope," 96.

76. Ibid.

77. Exceptions include Brown, *Religious Aesthetics*; González-Andrieu, *Bridge to Wonder*.

prehensive and systematic terms to theology that takes seriously context and histories particular to a faith community.[78] Elsewhere I have addressed my caution about borrowing from Schreiter, who is perhaps less aware of the complexity of what "local" means for racial/ethnic minority churches in the United States.[79] Local and global are closely interrelated in an increasingly globalized world. In a given community, people belong to multiple communities that are geographically distant. Nevertheless, the term *local* is useful in signaling the particular cultures, histories, and traditions that intersect at and define a place, even as a faith community's sense of what is local is contested and multiple.

My notion of LPTA is somewhat like James Hopewell's understanding of idiom, though he does not address aesthetics.[80] He understands idiom as "the language of a congregation" that reflects a process of imagination in which people negotiate metaphors, narratives, histories, and meanings that identify the congregation's life, its world, and God.[81] The language of a congregation consists of words, gestures, and artifacts that together convey the uniqueness of the congregation.[82] Hopewell's argument points to a creative, symbolic system for a congregation to communicate and reflect on its identity. LPTA specifies the preferred style in which this communication is achieved.

Clues to a community's LPTA are wherever the faithful experience a strong sense of God's beauty and where their imagination, creativity, and senses are most active.[83] A community's LPTA is often a mixture of aesthetics. A community can have an affinity for the performing arts, music, the visual arts, or the poetic word. They might sense God's beauty in feasting or in sacred architecture. Because communities have their own LPTA, each context needs different kinds of playing. When people are playing within and expanding the edges of their own LPTA, they are being true to themselves, which encourages expressions of true self. Fluency in LPTA enables people to feel at home, which is vital for playing.

78. Schreiter, *Constructing Local Theologies*.

79. Goto, "Asian American Practical Theologies," 281.

80. Hopewell, *Congregations*, 5.

81. Ibid.

82. Ibid.

83. For a comparison of congregational preferences for movement, see McFee, "Primal Patterns."

LPTA can speak movingly to a faith community to the extent to which they draw on and embody the community's history and theology. At spirit-filled African American churches, the aesthetic of worship involves singing, uninhibited improvisation in preaching, and spontaneous responses from the congregation. This aesthetic freedom is an experience of God's beauty for this community. It is also consistent with their yearning for spiritual freedom, characterized by the moving of Spirit. The God celebrated here is "the One who liberates and saves, delivering Daniel from the fiery furnace, Israel from Egypt's land, and prayer and praise from the shackles of rigid propriety."[84] Their style of worship creates a meaningful match between what is experienced in the form of worship and its theological content. LPTA in these churches speaks to and re-affirms an African American Christian sense of history and identity. For racial/ethnic minority churches whose sense of culture has been threatened, suppressed, or forgotten, culti-vating and claiming their LPTA would be vital.

LPTA makes sense in the body in the same way that other charac-teristics of habitus register in the body. More generally, *habitus* refers to systems of "structuring structures" that constitute an environment without obedience to rules or goals and collectively orchestrated without someone conducting them.[85] Habitus, which includes the aesthetics of a community, forms the body so that gestures, postures, and practices are a sensible, meaningful part of community life and identity. In community our sense of the sacred, as an existential encounter with otherness, is "phenomenologi-cally grounded in our embodiment."[86] For a musical church, glorifying God through music makes utter sense in the body, giving a person a feeling of ease and aliveness that is shared by others in the community. By attuning oneself to the body's wisdom and becoming aware of how LPTA appeals to the body, the faithful can learn to notice when they are playing and when they have been distracted from it. In other words, this kind of teaching can help people to listen for true self speaking through the body so that they might stay in the "sweet spot" of playing for the sake of faith. Experiences that resonate with a community's LPTA entice people to remain and sink into playing because it feels graceful.

84. Brown, *Religious Aesthetics*, 127.

85. Bourdieu, *Outline*, 72, 94.

86. Csordas, *Sacred Self*, 5.

Playing according to LPTA can assist the faithful in "sneaking up on God."[87] Open to surprise and wonder, playing within a faith community's LPTA helps people to lean into the new creation from their deep longings for what God has promised. At the same time, LPTA also provides clues as to how God is likely to sneak up on a faith community. It makes sense that revelatory experiencing happens in ways that resonate with LPTA. Surely God would not speak to a community of people in aesthetic ways they do not understand or to which they are not open.

DOING THEOLOGY BY PLAYING AESTHETICALLY

In tutoring the imagination, creativity, and the senses of the faithful, the good enough church (through good enough religious educators) form(s) people in the LPTA needed to participate in healthy illusions in the style of the community. For a visual arts church, this might mean teaching people to see connections between images and theology. For a musical church, this might entail teaching the faithful a deeper appreciation for music and theology, for a foodie church, food and theology. This kind of teaching and learning might involve experiential learning, critical reflection, and discussion. In addition, it would hopefully assist learners to perceive God's beauty more fully in experiences appropriate to their LPTA. By teaching the faithful to see, to hear, to feel, to smell, and to taste with greater sensitivity and acuity according to LPTA, people learn to attend to and appreciate their nuances. With greater mastery of their LPTA, the faithful are more able not only to grasp but also to create customized renditions of God's new creation. With enriched capacity, they can reconstruct the past, understand the present, and envision the future in light of their faith and communal stories. As the community develops its LPTA, it enriches and revitalizes its repertoire of renditions.

Daniël Louw argues that practical theological aesthetics enables a person to think in terms of metaphors and images, stimulating the imagination to come up with possibilities and images that give meaning to life, and create a world that can lead to the rediscovery of everyday experience.[88] One implication is that stimulating a church's LPTA can enable the community to think with theologically rich metaphors and images derived from their own aesthetic sensibilities. These metaphors can give the com-

87. Phil Porter interview with the author, June 12, 2008.

88. Louw, "Creative Hope," 99.

munity a means to express and to contemplate deep questions or issues that are important to the context.[89] (*The Garden Series* is an example of a church using a local metaphor to address conflict.) In addition, Louw argues that practical theological aesthetics must assist in reframing existing God-images. He writes, "[i]n practical theological aesthetics, imagination should therefore toy with new images which can portray God in terms of contextuality."[90] This suggests that nurturing a community's LPTA helps to facilitate playing with God images. A new God image to contemplate might be more likely to be understood and appreciated if it resonates with the community's LPTA. Furthermore, LPTA can assist a community to play with new images of themselves as a people of God, as in the case of *The Garden Series*. A community can draw upon LPTA to give form to what needs transformation.

As important as it is for a community to be versed and immersed in LPTA, expanding them is equally valuable. LPTA allows the faithful to appreciate God's beauty in forms beyond what is familiar and to appreciate diverse renditions of God's new creation. They help people grasp and create a wider range of theologically rich images and metaphors, increasing their ability to consider unfamiliar God images and to reflect on contextual issues with greater complexity. Expanding LPTA can increase possibilities for expressiveness and creativity, which opens avenues for new and provocative experiences of Christians playing.

89. Ibid.
90. Ibid.

chapter 6

TOWARDS A NEW CREATION

One might say that "Persons know grace who do not know grace *as* grace. . . . To be sure, the mission of the church is in part to increase the number of persons who know grace as grace."[1] Knowing "grace *as* grace" helps the faithful to be open to, to detect, to reflect on, and to be transformed by grace more deeply. Therefore, the church endeavors to help people by giving them symbols to know consciously the grace they know with the fullness of their being. The same can be said of this book. I have labored to assist readers to know the grace of playing explicitly by providing concepts, terms, and insights about processes of playing.

I took up the challenge of exploring how religious educators might engage learners in revelatory experiencing, which forms people in relating to one another more deeply and thereby allows them to create and be created anew. My strategy has been to offer the language of playing to open up to view what is being created together in revelatory experiencing, which at times religious educators and learners know by feel but may not have brought to critical reflection. The language of playing has provided terms and concepts for symbolizing some of the felt senses to which revelatory experiencing also points. The notion of playing has lent richness, depth, and empirical evidence toward developing a theory of facilitating revelatory experiencing. By being introduced to some analytic tools to recognize the familiar, perhaps it has been surprising to realize how often we experience the felt sense that playing and revelatory experiencing each symbolize in part. While not a focus of the work, a side benefit has also been to see how revelatory diverse forms of playing can be, perhaps bringing to awareness

1. Gustafson, *Ethics*, 118.

114

the creativity and graciousness of Spirit and the many opportunities for partnership.

This practical theological project has required various strategies and diverse conversation partners from cognate disciplines. Because the territory of revelatory experiencing is mysterious, varied, and not easily encompassed, an interdisciplinary approach was necessary. I offered multiple perspectives from which to view playing—psychoanalytic, theological, and historical. Then I argued for adding a fourth, an aesthetic perspective. Each of the four perspectives made unique contributions to understanding playing. In addition, juxtaposing psychoanalytic, theological, historical, and aesthetic perspectives against one another allowed each to serve as a complement and a corrective to the others, revealing what each highlights and mutes in understanding playing. At the same time, this interdisciplinary conversation involved theory that sheds light on practices of playing *and* cases of communal playing that bring new insight to theory. Finally, this project drew analogies between past and present communities who experience the grace of playing, while keeping an eschatological eye on the future. All of this made for a complex undertaking.

In this final chapter, I offer an example of a performance artist playing with inmates in a detention center to explore when, where, and with whom playing happens for love's sake in everyday life. Paired with the Japanese American church in Sacramento, playing in a detention center creates symmetry with the playing of medieval nuns and fools, who represent playing within ecclesial institutions and in everyday life. All of these examples suggest not only that playing for the sake of faith *can* happen anywhere and anytime, but also that playing *needs* to happen in as many times and places as possible for all of creation to move toward the fullness of what God intends.

In what follows, the four perspectives on playing outlined in previous chapters highlight the significance of revelatory experiencing among young men incarcerated in a place that appears to be God forsaken but is not. The example tells how grace appears in the midst of playing with those who suffer personal, communal, and historic wounds. While this was true of members of the Japanese American church, the detention center involves playing that reaches toward strangers who are invisible to those with power and privilege, not strangers within the same community (as was the case in the last chapter). With the analysis, I intend to demonstrate how these four perspectives on playing can be used to mine critically one's own teaching and the many contexts that religious education takes place. I conclude by synthesizing more succinctly and systematically key ideas presented in earlier chapters to garner fresh insights for a theory of facilitating revelatory experiencing that makes clear why it is morally and spiritually important.

PLAYING IN A DETENTION CENTER

Masankho Banda, a performance artist, healer, and teacher, tells the story of playing with inmates of San Francisco's Juvenile Detention Center, Cell Block H, where the worst offenders are incarcerated. He recounted the story.

> I went in and I said, "My name is Masankho Banda and I'm here to sing and dance with you."
>
> "Why?" looking at me like, "If you don't give me a good answer, I'm going to take your head off. I don't have a gun, so I can't cap you but I'll take your head off."
>
> And I said, "Because I care about you and I love you."
>
> "You don't care jack. You don't even know me."
>
> I said, "Yes, I don't know you but I don't have to know you. All I know is that right now you and I are standing in this place." I said, "What's your name?" He told me. He was a[n Asian] young man . . . I said, "Where do you live?"
>
> He told me an address somewhere in the Mission [District]. And I started to sing just based on his name and his address and what I could see of his appearance. He went from leaning back, disinterested, to sitting up and looking at me.[2]

Masankho went on to describe how he created eight songs for eight different young men. As a result, they said to him, "Nobody has even said to us that they love us. Nobody has taken the time." And they said, "How did you know all of that about me?" Masankho interpreted the significance of the story, saying,

> I know that in that moment God was there. In that moment there was a sense in my core being and knowing that I was reaching these kids on a level at which no lecture [or] book would be able to.
>
> No, I don't know the kids. . . . It was only a one-time session. I didn't go back to them. Who knows? Maybe they left there and as soon as they were out went and car jacked another car. . . . But I

2. Masankho Banda interview with the author, June 20, 2008.

would like to think that of the . . . eight or twelve kids that were in there that one of them went back to his cell and said, "What was that about? What was that about?"[3]

Masankho was engaged in a pedagogy of playing that was both surprising and decentering for these young men. His hope was that his playing with them might create some kind of awakening or opening to love and to the divine.

ANALYSIS FROM FOUR PERSPECTIVES ON PLAYING

As I stated at the beginning of this volume, revelatory experiencing involves re-orienting encounters that give rise to a shift in awareness or feeling in learners because they have related to one another more deeply or truly. Just as it did for *The Garden Series*, the four perspectives on playing (psychoanalytic, theological, historical and aesthetic) indicate some of what is being created in revelatory experiencing, including what the inmates might have created. To appreciate the context of the story, I will start with a historically-minded account.

Masanhko's story is set in San Francisco's Juvenile Detention Center, a short-term facility that serves an urban area. Despite attempts to reform the city's juvenile justice system, African American and Latino male youth continue to suffer the highest rates of detention and recidivism.[4] Historically, these young men tend to come from neighborhoods that experience high rates of violence and gang activity.[5] Between 1995 and 2005, the rate of detention for White and Asian youth (male and female) at this facility decreased by 52.4 percent and 41.0 percent, respectively, while the detention rate for Latino youth declined by only 0.1 percent and increased by 9.3 percent for African American youth.[6] When arrested, African American youth are almost three times more likely to be detained in San Francisco's juvenile justice system than a white youth, and a Latino youth nearly six times more likely.[7] With these kinds of statistics, one can imagine why detainees would not expect to play and/or to be loved by a stranger.

3. Ibid.

4. San Francisco Juvenile Probation Department, "Program Narrative."

5. Ibid.

6. This refers to youth ages ten to seventeen, per 100,000 population. Center on Juvenile and Criminal Justice, "Juvenile Detention."

7. Ibid., 8–9.

One can also understand this example of revelatory experiencing in light of Winnicott's approach to playing. In his theory, from the earliest years of playing, baby experiences being cared for by being held, seen, and fed from the breast or bottle. In some ways, Masankho was holding these young men in his seeing and his singing, creating intimacy through sound, breath, and sight. He was acting in such a way that was reminiscent of a good enough mother, who mirrors baby's creative gestures for the sake of his/her growth and wellbeing. In a sense, Masankho was intentionally acting in ways such that the young men could experience him as nurturing and supporting their tiny, tentative gestures of willingness to play and reflecting them back with compassion.

Winnicott argues that "mirroring" is a key practice that fosters the infant's creativity, even before being presented with a transitional object. In being held and handled satisfactorily, the baby sees him or herself in the mother's face, as if looking in a mirror. According to Winnicott, when the mother is looking at the baby, "what she looks like is related to what she sees there."[8] For example, a baby smiles and the mother smiles back. Striving to be seen (first by mother and then by others), writes Winnicott, is the basis of "creative looking."[9] Over a lifetime, an individual undergoes a long process that depends on being seen: "When I look I am seen, so I exist. I can now afford to look and see. I now look creatively and what I apperceive I also perceive. In fact, I take care not to see what is not there to be seen (unless I am tired)."[10] Having been seen and known, ideally a person is empowered to look at the world creatively and expect the world to respond positively to what she creates. Unfortunately, not everyone enjoys proper mirroring in the family and/or in society, which is the case for marginalized people. Winnicott gives several cases from his practice of adult clients struggling to be seen in a way that makes them feel they exist.

Masankho's playing with these young men is not so different from a good therapist acting in ways that help a client feel that he/she is being seen. An analyst makes an inference about a client's inner world and gives it back in the form of an image, a metaphor, or a story, ideally capturing what is essential in the person's lived experience.[11] In Masankho's case, the songs potentially functioned as what Winnicott called a subjective object,

8. Winnicott, *Playing and Reality*, 151.

9. Ibid., 154.

10. Ibid.

11. Wright, *Mirroring and Attunement*, 35.

which originates from beyond the baby/young man yet can be "taken in" and incorporated. Each song was created for a particular inmate to "have" or keep as his own. As in a therapeutic setting, what is given back to the client feels new because the form gives the person a means to perceive his/her experience as never before.[12] At the detention center, the songs were potentially powerful because they were intended to (and perhaps in some cases able to) embody something true about the inmate, which he did not consciously communicate. In addition, the songs were given in an unlikely place, where one would not expect to be seen or known. In a place where one's humanity is hidden, having a song that conveys a sense that "I see you" could be a gift of grace. In Masankho's country of origin, Malawi, to say "hello" is to communicate "I see you." For his part, he could only act and relate with intention to play with the young men, creating possibilities for experiencing something meaningful together. However, what each person was able to create, discover, and take in was primarily determined in the space between him and Masankho. The same was true of my mother and each member of her congregation that experienced *The Garden Series*.

From a theological standpoint, Masankho could be interpreted as having intended to tap into the infinite possibilities presented by Spirit, participating in Spirit's creativity that is ever present. In the moment, he sensed what the young men needed in order to hear and then to create what was gracious, novel, and transformative. Masankho said, "I had to really key in and listen to the energy exchange that was going on with these young men as I sang to them. And improvisation allows that even more than if they had filled out a questionnaire for me to sing from."[13] If he had known some facts about these young men ahead of time, said Masankho, he would have formed mental categories that likely would have diminished his ability to create these powerful songs. Though one can never completely bracket one's mental categories, Masankho intentionally practiced being open to what was emerging in the space between him and the young men. In perceiving subtle cues in the moment of improvisation, Masankho gave back a sense of the person, but in a loving form. In effect, Masankho was partnering with Spirit to reveal a new way of being and being together.

One can also understand this story as testament to playing that allows people to practice more life-giving ways of thinking, feeling, and doing. Masankho's playing with these young men decentered their habitual patterns

12. Ibid.
13. Banda, interview.

of being, which not only allowed but also sought to open them up to an alternative. He was constructing a "counter-environment" that allowed these young men to live into what we might understand to be God's new creation, in which those who are on the margins are loved and redeemed.[14] He also demonstrates what Moltmann calls "being-with/for-others" in our playing, which is being in solidarity and in relationship with those who are oppressed and not seen as valuable members of society.

From an aesthetic perspective, Masankho was not only constructing a counter-environment, he was offering a rendition of each young man, portraying each person as a child of God within each song. Although Masankho's renditions were ephemeral, they were no less powerful in intending to speak intimately to each person, yet his approach was rooted in a community. His renditions drew not only from the artist's repertoire, but the aesthetic resources of the InterPlay community, of which Masankho is a part.[15] In the local practical theological aesthetics of InterPlay, participants regularly experience what co-founder Phil Porter calls "God moments" that happen spontaneously in the midst of creative improvisation. Masankho reached out to the detainees using the LPTA of the communities from which he came.

Masankho was also teaching body-to-body. His physical presence in the detention center was itself a lesson, by embodying love in a place where most cannot and dare not go. The songs were not sacred in the traditional sense, but they were intended as healing songs nonetheless, conveying more than musical sound but also meaning that was deeper than even the lyrics. The songs conveyed a gesture that Masankho communicated physically, symbolically, and aesthetically.

These four perspectives on Masankho's playing—as seen from psychoanalytic, theological, historical, and aesthetic points of view—are not simply parallel accounts. They intersect one another. In this example, if one attends to the historical context and the aesthetics of the detention center, one sees how Masankho was able to interrupt a history of hopelessness and a sterile environment with LPTA that came from elsewhere, communicating attentiveness, spontaneity, and joy. If one focuses on the psychological and theological implications of Masankho's intervention, one gains insight about how authentic, creative, and courageous contact with other human beings can help God's presence be felt and known. If one reflects on the

14. See chapter 3, n. 42 above.
15. Goto, "Artistic Play."

historical, psychological, and theological perspectives on the story, one realizes that human beings are able to participate in the grace of playing, at least to some degree, even if their agency has been historically or is presently limited.

USING THE TOOLS, FINDING INSPIRATION FOR TEACHING

While revelatory experiencing occurs with and without critical reflection, the four perspectives on playing (psychoanalytic, theological, historical, and aesthetic) are a set of analytic tools that can be used to bring to light the grace that instigates and accompanies revelatory experiencing. In reflecting on one's own teaching, one might discover that some of one's best teaching moments are revelatory and can be critically reflected upon in terms of playing. This set of analytic tools can help to explain how and why learners and teachers are at times open, engaged, creative and transformed by being together and with Spirit.

From these four perspectives on how and why playing happens, one can also infer why playing fails to happen on some occasions of religious education. There might be contextual and historical reasons why playing is easier or more difficult. Leaders may or may not be acting in ways that allow diverse members of a group to experience them as good enough mothers, who are able to see and respond to what is needed by the community. A local church may be more or less able to function as a good enough mother and be an environment conducive to authentic relating and creative engagement. A faith community may be more or less open to seeing or experiencing themselves and/or God as playing. It may be easier or more difficult for some communities to value decentering experiences that come with playing and to form people in taking risks for the sake of faith. To one degree or another, a community may or may not be able to draw readily upon their aesthetic and cultural resources to play with the deep questions of their hearts or to help others to play. Whatever the case, these four perspectives on playing can help indicate the area(s) in which a community might need assistance.

Despite all that can go wrong, some of the grace of playing is that revelatory experiencing often happens despite obstacles. The detention center did not have a history of openness or a communal memory of playing. Probably the detainees did not see themselves as playing children of

God. The young men were not accustomed to taking the kind of personal risks that Masankho was inviting them to experience. However, he created conditions that invited the young men to create with him, and in doing so they might experience him as a caring, good enough parent. Masankho drew on aesthetic and cultural resources of his communities to create a temporary place of playing. This suggests that conditions need not be perfect. All historic, psychoanalytic, theological, and aesthetic factors need not be aligned for learners to enjoy revelatory experiencing. By the grace of God, the environment need only be good enough. Spirit seeks and attempts to find us despite the challenges.

There is no blueprint for facilitating revelatory experiencing because no two opportunities for religious education are alike and because the complexity of playing makes it impossible to prescribe. However, using these analytic tools, one might recognize in retrospect how and why some teaching moments flowered into revelatory experiencing and others did not. In addition, these tools might be used in anticipation of more graceful teaching in the future by weaving together psychoanalytic, theological, historical, and aesthetic views of playing and considering if and how one can create conditions for playing. Below I illustrate some familiar contexts of religious education including playing in a classroom, in a liturgical setting, and in everyday life—all of which are enriched by the grace of playing. The examples are intended to be evocative rather than exhaustive. Made more complex by the integration of the four analytic tools, they provide further points of reference and inspiration for creative envisioning of learning.

In a classroom where learners first meet as strangers to one another, playing begins with building a community of learners who are willing to take risks with one another—to dare to be seen and known perhaps in ways that are unfamiliar to themselves and in the presence of others. This is crucial to the community's ability to lean into challenging ideas, new ways of relating, and alternative ways of envisioning possibilities. It starts with good enough religious educators taking risks and enticing others to join them. Like the holy fools, Masankho made himself vulnerable to the possibility of being threatened and rejected. However, any teacher takes similar risks in laying bare his/her passionate and sometimes still nascent ideas for learners to play with. At the same time, learners must feel safe enough to risk being creative and authentic with their own insights and responses, offering what may feel untested in sharing what matters. A psychoanalytic view of playing suggests that the teacher must be authentic in his/her playing in order to invite and engage learners to play along. Baby cannot play without mother's initiative, response, and genuine participation.

From the riches of his/her creative repertoire, the teacher fashions renditions of subject matter for learners to take up, examine, revise, and use as material for their own renditions. How a teacher renders a subject will partly depend on the historical, theological, and cultural context where learning is taking place. The good enough religious educator provides opportunities, encouragement, and modeling for learners to create with the material—sometimes critically, sometimes metaphorically, other times aesthetically. An educator might teach and invite learners to create in ways that *build* on the local practical theological aesthetics of the institution offering the class, or in ways that *expand* LPTA. Educators do this differently. Some prefer challenging texts, some narratives, others music, others silence, others video, and still others movement. Some facilitate playing well within the LPTA of their institution, while others prefer dabbling at the edge, inviting learners to register and be thoughtful about what they are experiencing.

The content of classroom learning is not simply material to be absorbed or received, but to be taken up, played with, and re-created. *The point is to enter with others into interactive, participatory relationship with content given by Christian and/or other tradition(s) through the creative process.* At the same time, learners and teachers are being formed into a faith community as they depend on one another for inspiration, mirroring, and the flow of movement between creativity and imagination. In moments of playing, the teacher is not the central source of knowledge, to whom all learners are connecting. Rather, learners and teachers are "living an experience together," through multiple, simultaneous connections that grow organically as people explore possibilities of the content provided. Both the content and the process are meant to form the faithful in embodying the message of love in creative, often courageous ways of being.

When teaching in a classroom, religious educators engage learners in subject matter to create what is new, all the while creating conditions for true self to come alive and participate in the playing. The learning community (individually and collaboratively) creates renditions from class material that become takeaways—be it a memory, a memento, or in some contexts class notes or a paper. In a Christian context, the learning community becomes a rendition of the learning body of Christ, which changes and adapts each time the class is constituted. As a body of Christ, the learning community opens itself up to being formed by encounters with Spirit.

Spirit might surprise members of the learning community in their discoveries, their aliveness, their sharing, and their creativity. The grace of playing in a classroom can feel especially gracious because it happens too rarely in all the years of schooling a person typically experiences.

In a liturgical or ritual setting, playing immerses learners in the history and traditions of the community by inviting them to participate in the drama of a play world rich with religious meaning. Like the classroom, good enough religious educators offer a plethora of materials (in this case, the language, the symbols, and gestures) with which to engage. Both the classroom and the context of liturgy provide structure for playing. While traditional materials and structure for playing may be rich in and of themselves, what is most important is helping leaners to create with the materials and with one another. Believers need opportunities, permission, and guidance to imagine and to create anew with the stuff of tradition. They need to be able to construct their own renditions that recapture and re-present the wisdom of the sacred texts. For Christians, each person must deepen connections to one another and to God with the help of the community, by creating a Jesus to dress up and take home, just as the Rheinland nuns did.

In the last chapter, *The Garden Series* was an example of a church using local resources to create visual renditions in the drama of faith, but more often this same creativity happens in the play of preaching.[16] A preacher takes what has been given by tradition, but also creates with materials derived from the congregation's own context, history, and theology, including narratives, images, and symbols. When these materials from people's lives are woven into a sermon, they have the power to beckon the faithful with an irresistible invitation to play, taking them to their particular growing edge of faith. This is heightened if the sermon is performed according to the LPTA of the community so that the style of the performance matches what the congregation finds most compelling. In receiving the sermon, the faithful are invited to "make" what they can from the sermon. In both cases of preaching and liturgical art, what is given by tradition can be made anew with materials from a community's context(s), rather than assuming that what is given is appropriate in all times and places or that it comes without a context. Renditions in preaching and liturgical art make palpable and more real contextualized understandings of the gospel. They cohere with and at times build upon communal traditions of rendering the good news, ensuring that they hit home in addressing what is needed for faith forma-

16. Jones, *Jazz of Preaching.*

tion and discipleship. Whether visual, oral, musical, gustatory, or olfactory, renditions fashioned from the community's stores allow the faithful to sense who God is, who they are meant to be as God's people, and what response is called for in this time and place.

In liturgical contexts and elsewhere, religious educators help the faithful to create as they find the God that they need. The notion of "creating God" might sound outrageous and maybe even blasphemous, but at some level God is discovered in the creating, yet is already there to be found. Just as baby "creates" the object that baby needs, the faithful render the God they need for more abundant living. A person attributes to God her highest values, such as love, strength, and wisdom, as well as her worst fears.[17] At the same time, God remains beyond human need or creativity, far exceeding an individual or communal perspective, experience, or capacity. In Christian traditions, the biblical text witnesses to One who has acted from the beginning of creation and continues to act in human history and everyday life. To capture some of who God is, the faithful need to play with what has been given by tradition in connection with their lives.[18]

Doing what invites playing in liturgy may be more challenging than classroom teaching. In the Protestant tradition, educators are often called upon to breathe life into liturgy that has become dry and perfunctory. They help learners be open to revelatory experiencing even if the performance of liturgy is familiar and practiced. Temporarily heightening the aesthetic dimensions of a practice in startling or dramatic ways and inviting people to contemplate their experience can aid in tutoring imagination and the senses. For example, leading communion in darkness at a pastors' retreat can help participants to experience the familiar in new ways.[19] As practiced as Christian clergy are with serving and receiving communion, they might experience this liturgy anew by having to do it by feel and by ear alone. The text of the liturgy has not been changed. The experience of taking communion in the dark may resemble how a blind person would experience it. However, for the sighted, darkness can be an evocative overlay that sparks imagination and the senses to perceive mystery afresh. When learners return to liturgy with the lights on, they might have gained insight, bodily memory, and/or relationships with others that bring new awareness to the practice.

17. Ulanov, *Finding* Space, 33.

18. Ibid., 14.

19. Proposed by my students at the Boston University School of Theology.

With the help of Spirit, good enough religious educators within liturgical contexts (and elsewhere) create facilitating environments that invite people *to participate in imagining and to some degree embodying God's new* creation. In partnership with those who plan and lead liturgy, Spirit moves the faithful to creative engagement with sacred objects, images, and practices that invite new ways of being and being with one another. Like all practices that foster transformation, sometimes playing is neither necessarily quick nor finished. Some playing results from committed, habitual returning, as is the case with a sacrament, a class, or an ongoing program. Other times, playing arises from a one-time event, as was true of *The Garden Series*, which was created in response to a specific need or opportunity. It takes faithfulness to "show up" to play, to create space for encounters with Spirit, and to anticipate revelatory experiencing without pre-determining it, predicting it, or being disappointed if it does not happen.

In addition to classroom and liturgical contexts, religious educators can and do facilitate playing in everyday life with greater intention. A dancer is drawn to investigate music she hears within a deserted university chapel, where a man unknown to her is improvising on the piano. They have no shared history, but the chapel is holy place, traditionally a safe place. She is a religious educator who has used movement improvisation in her teaching and is visiting the campus. He is a musician and an arborist taking a break from his job. Without introductions, she begins to dance to his music, and to her delight he continues to make music. As long as he plays, she dances and as long as she dances, he plays. Without words they rejoice in discovering their shared aesthetic sensibilities, lingering in the beauty of improvisation. Another man praying in the chapel moves closer to witness the duet. Although all three are moved and exhilarated by playing together, they will never meet again. Spirit is palpable though unnamed.

Elsewhere, a church group with therapy dogs visits a local veterans hospital. The dogs invite the men to play, and they are drawn irresistibly into petting, talking to, and creating what they most need by interacting with the dogs. For those who have been wounded by the trauma of war, touching and being touched playfully or lovingly by a living being who asks little imparts a sense of aliveness. In addition, the dogs provide the occasion for handlers to speak to those whom they have never met. They talk about the dog and sometimes other stories are shared. For the vets, the grace of playing comes not only in being seen and "known" by a friendly dog, but also being seen and known indirectly by the handlers, who create the space of playing and provide a loving, living "toy" to play and be with. The dog mediates the encounter between humans, providing an easy way of relating to one another. This too is bit of playing at/in the God's new creation, where hope and delight are no small gifts in the face of aging, infirmity, wounded memory, and the end of life.

The prospect of playing in everyday life challenges religious educators to consider how we invite others into playing if we have never met before. They may not share our history, theology, culture, or familiarity with the ways that people of faith play. They may not have been tutored in the healthy illusions of the faith community/ies to which we belong. In public, the invitation to play must be made do-able, recognizable, and compelling. The structure of playing must be signaled in such a way that players feel safe enough to be creative and spontaneous. In making playing accessible, we are in fact meeting people where they are, even as we invite them to enter the illusionistic play world being offered. Good enough religious educators provide hospitality for all to play, including strangers. Recall that this is the way of Jesus, inviting those who are on the margins, to venture and play in order to have greater abundance.

Wherever religious educators teach formally or informally, including in everyday life, they have at their disposal personal and communal repertoires with which to facilitate playing. They are grounded in their ability to form community by encouraging others' creativity, which requires the teachers' own knowledge of self, confidence, and creativity. Religious educators adapt and sometimes translate what they have to offer to the learning context, whenever it may arise, according to the needs of the moment.

FORMING LEARNERS FOR DECENTERING AND RE-CENTERING

In these last few sections, I would like to express more succinctly insights for a theory of facilitating revelatory experiencing. If revelation involves God "interrupting" the course of human history,[20] revelatory experiencing involves little "interruptions" in which we participate with God in the new creation. What is being interrupted is the way in which people normally relate to one another, and in doing so engage reality and one another differently. This resonates with the insight that revelation (especially in everyday forms) is experienced in the "in between" of the "meeting" between per-

20. Boeve, *God Interrupts History*.

sons, humans and the world, and humans and God.[21] The meeting is what interrupts or decenters, graciously opening us up to grace.

The language of playing lends insight about how God is revealed unexpectedly in the midst of relating to one another, though we may not consciously seek it. One could say that the in-between space of revelatory experiencing is the everyday stage for human being and becoming in the drama of faith, which emerges mysteriously when we are playing. In playing, we forget ourselves as individuals, which paradoxically makes us more open to what is larger than ourselves, including others and Spirit. It is there that the spaces between human beings, humans and the world, and humans and God are charged with potential, creativity, and freedom. Winnicott refers to "potential space." In this in-between space, relationships formed in playing are life-giving and sometimes transformative, altering at least temporarily and at times profoundly people's ways of being with one another. In Christian traditions, the faithful do not know the good news simply because they have read or been told about it. They experience it in relating to others, knowing it in their bodies, with the senses, in heartfelt imaginings, and authentic exchanges that hit home. When abundance, love, and grace that the Bible conveys are lived with others, this is what is revelatory. Playing is one means by which we experience Christ's way as liberating, surprising, timeless, and timely.

As we experience ways of being and being together that have not yet become habitual, the process of playing and leaning into who God intends us to be and be with-and-for-others is revealing both to ourselves and to others. However, revelatory experiencing is even more complex and mysterious than that. In revelatory experiencing, the Holy One—who plays and who is willing to seek and find us—is revealed in the hide-and-seek of being and becoming human. Furthermore, our connections to one another and to Spirit are revealed in playing. As some of us play in Christian communities, we sense more fully ourselves as an interrelated people who need one another to play at/in the new creation. Not only is our dependence on one another made more apparent, playing for the sake of faith in the present connects us to the playing of God's people who have gone before—biblical figures, medieval saints, and creative teachers who have marked Christian history. Through diverse pedagogies of playing, the creative seeking of believers past and present serves as testimony to the faithful partnering of Spirit.

21. See chapter 1, n. 15 above.

At least at first, the relationships involved in playing are decentering. Yet paradoxically, they are ultimately the means by which learners are able to tolerate and maybe even be inspired to welcome decentering. As people relate to one another in more authentic and spontaneous ways in playing, this itself is a departure from the norms of non-playing. Moreover, relating to others through playing can also disturb what is unexamined or taken-for-granted within individuals and communities. In Christian contexts, sometimes what is destabilized can be as invisible as assumptions about who has power, which bodies matter, who God is, and what counts as church. Other times what is disrupted is as apparent as where learning happens, what worship looks like, and how Christians and others normally act. None of these is a small or insignificant pattern to interrupt, and any one of them might keep people hostage. However, the relationships formed in playing make the decentering tolerable and sometimes profound as people lean together into what is unfamiliar, challenging, or wondrous.

Openness to being decentered with one another is a spiritual posture that playing at/in the new creation fosters in learners. This is markedly different than education that emphasizes the transmission of historical facts, for example, about Jesus' life and the context in which he lived. Openness to being decentered also contrasts with the transmission of right belief, which can give both teachers and learners a sense of security, assurance, or autonomy. Acquiring facts or believing rightly involves no one but the believer because it is a matter of individual choice and commitment to know or believe. However, pedagogies of playing for love's sake are interpersonal, often revealing what learners most need to know in being with others. Playing is hardly for the faint of heart because relating deeply to others demands more of us. Sometimes playing invites people to do, be seen, or to say as they have never done and could not do without support. Some learners will appropriately resist playing because living with histories of racism, sexism, homophobia, or other forms of prejudice require them to be wary of being vulnerable with others. Others will avoid playing because it often disturbs patterns of power and privilege, which they cannot imagine living without. However, with the help of a good enough religious educator many learners come to trust that the gains from playing together are worth more than the risks and vulnerability required.

Hope summons learners to tolerate the risks of playing. The nuns and fools dedicated themselves to Christ in ways that were often misunderstood and disparaged by others, yet they were lured by the hope of being closer to

Christ. For the first time the Garden Angels were moved to speak publicly about their faith, hoping that their participation in *The Garden Series* would help the congregation heal from conflict. Young men at the detention center were summoned to play with Masankho, hoping that maybe—just maybe—he would treat them differently than others had. Students, preachers, and teachers routinely risk their ideas, hoping that their offering will enliven the community's learning and growing. A pianist keeps playing for a dancer he does not know, hoping his music is a gift. Vets in the hospital play with dogs, accepting a gift from strangers, hoping that they might receive some measure of comfort or companioning even if only for a little while. People know that there is potential goodness in playing. As much as they are able, they hope, trust, and risk even though they cannot predict fully what goodness is in store or how they might feel in receiving it, given the fact that goodness comes in many forms. Hope is a gift of Spirit—as is the grace of playing. When hope is met with the grace of playing, learners become more open to the risks, even if it means being de-centered.

Pedagogies of playing at/in God's new creation place high demands on learners, but also on the teacher(s). The risks to the religious educator in teaching through pedagogies of playing are real but perhaps not unfamiliar. In order for learners to play, both psychically and aesthetically the teacher must set up the environment for playing so that learners will know where and how to enter the spaces in which creating and authentic relating can happen. Whether implicitly or explicitly, the teacher must also make sensible the pedagogy of playing historically, contextually, and theologically so that the "why" of playing helps learners feel safe enough. Failing to do any of these well can result in learners refusing to play or not being able to play as well as they might. Perhaps most risky of all is that the educator must be willing to play with learners, which often upsets expectations about the roles of both teacher and learners. Playing requires the teacher to be open to being decentered in the midst of teaching, which means daring to be creative, modeling authenticity, and dealing with unexpected emotions and insights as creativity and imagination blossom in the process. Not only are learners being seen and known in new ways, so too the teacher might well be. Religious educators are familiar with the vulnerability, spontaneity, flexibility, and courage that good teaching requires. Just as learners are not risking for naught, religious educators risk for the possibility that learners will know revelatory experiencing. While there are risks to both learners and teachers alike, falling short of playing in teaching and learning takes its toll on communities and individuals as people feel less and less alive or real.

The decentering that happens in playing does not simply end with disruption but with re-centering—settling not in the same place as one started but in a different one. The goal is not simply to decenter learners but also to help learners find new axes for centering that give more life. All four analytic tools I have presented reinforce the importance of re-centering that can come as result of playing. First, from a psychoanalytic perspective, Winnicott addressed a potential shift in perspective when he theorizes about the role of object destruction in playing. As discussed in the case of devotional dolls, only if a transitional object were destroyed (and in doing so, one's idea of reality were impinged upon), would there be an opportunity to gain a new perspective on reality because what the object represents has "survived." Second, from a historical perspective, the spirited, back-and-forth play of exchange in Socratic method or teaching in Hebrew tradition, which involves questioning and challenging the learner, encourages the learner to re-see and revise what was perhaps taken for granted. Third, from a theological perspective, Jesus creatively used stories, questions, and metaphors to decenter people's thinking so that they could construct fresh images and ideas of God's new creation. The disciples were not passively receiving Jesus' wisdom, but rather they accepted the responsibility for engaging what he taught, wrestling with it, and being open to the possibility of it transforming them radically. Fourth, from an aesthetic perspective, playing recruits the imagination and the senses so that we might be absorbed in the space of playing. The world cannot help but look and feel different—perhaps richer—for us having played together.

THE GRACE OF PLAYING IN WORLDS IN NEED

Worlds abound where true self does not feel at home, and this is where the transformative, healing creativity of Spirit is needed. Where freedom and authenticity are impinged upon—whether in families, in schools, in workplaces, churches, or elsewhere—true self will not play because it is not safe. Where there is silence, alienation, and brokenness between people, true self remains hidden and protected. Where there is dehumanization, prejudice, and marginalization, true self dare not express itself. The youth detention center that Masankho visited is a place where all of this is seen starkly. However, more often than not and to one degree or another, we live in worlds of need, where true self is hiding and waiting, longing to be sought, found, and lovingly enticed to emerge more frequently. In houses of worship, in lecture halls, and in cubicles, faithful people (including ourselves at times) spend more time hiding our true thoughts and feelings, numbed out, and conforming to what is expected rather than leaning into the reality to which God's new creation beckons us. Wherever false self bides time in bastions of compliance and complacency, patterns that maintain the status quo continue unchallenged, with individuals and communities remaining captive. With so many waiting in the many worlds of which we are a part, teaching that interrupts, evokes, and inspires is needed more than ever for the sake of God's new creation.

A good enough religious educator helps the faithful to approach in mediated form some of what they need to grow. In being seen and known in the process of playing, one can dare to seek and find indirectly some of what one needs for transformation as well as hope to be sought and found. With the participation of others, playing can be a means of restoring, recreating, or symbolizing what has been loved or needed but lost, neglected, or damaged in the process of living.[22] Sometimes a metaphor, an image, or an object can be sought and found and thereby created, which helps a learner to shift toward greater abundance by disrupting and expanding what was previously known. Other times, grace simply comes in the experience of creating together what one could not have been imagined or created alone. Approaching indirectly some of what is needed for transformation is an active process of seeking in hope and faith, knowing by heart and in one's bones what God has done and promised.

Despite the high level of human participation in revelatory experiencing, what is revealed is not revealed *from* teacher *to* learner but *between* teacher and leaner and *among* all members of the learning community. It dawns unexpectedly, and therefore one cannot seek outright what will come as a graceful surprise. Even the most gifted teacher cannot tell a learner definitively what she needs to learn in order to make a shift toward wholeness, but he/she can provide structure, content, and space to explore and create. A good enough religious educator can provide hospitality and support needed for the creative process. At the same time, a learner can show up with openness, hope, and the courage to reach for what is good but not fully known. A seeker can learn to see beyond what is literal and to sense life-giving possibilities that evoke, haunt, and shape the imagination

22. Milner, *Paint*, 67.

and the senses, propelling a person to feel toward Spirit's calling for her life. A learner can become practiced at listening for true self "speaking" through the "bodyspirit,"[23] indicating when playing allows one to approach what one needs. As a child of God, a person can become accustomed to trusting Spirit's pull toward goodness—what feels urgent, deep, and momentous in playing. Drawing near to what is translucent, authentic, and vulnerable can evoke a range of emotions, which is why playing together requires trusting Spirit as well as fellow players.

In supporting people to become themselves, Parker Palmer argues for the necessity of giving up "fixing, saving, advising, and setting each other straight," but such habits are hard to break for well-intended people.[24] At best, he says, "My answer to your deepest difficulties merely reflects what I would do if I were you, which I am not."[25] In fact, fixing or advising benefits the teacher's ego more than anything.[26] Playing grants greater agency to the learner than teaching based on a schooling model or authoritarian approaches to learning. Pedagogies of playing involve trusting and supporting the learner to create what is good from what is offered from the community's wisdom and traditions, which itself can be experienced by learners as loving and empowering. Learners come to experience themselves as good enough creators who are able to seek and find by creating with Spirit what matters in the moment.

Just as individuals bring their own wounds and limitations to playing, Christian and other faith communities show up for playing with limiting patterns and distinctive wounds that hinder the faithful from living together as God intends. Communities have internalized histories of racism, homophobia, trauma, and other unexamined issues that shape a community's theological and moral orientation, behavior, and being. Helping a community play with what limits its members is an act of love, just as it was in the case of my mother and *The Garden Series*. It requires great courage and creativity to help a community approach indirectly what troubles or wounds them, especially when people are heavily or unconsciously invested in problematic patterns of being. If one attempts to tackle limitations or wounds too directly,[27] the community may balk as individuals can and

23. Winton-Henry and Porter, *What the Body Wants*.

24. Palmer, *Hidden Wholeness*, 116.

25. Ibid.

26. Ibid.

27. Informal conversations with Cynthia Winton-Henry and Phil Porter.

do. False self remains on guard. Rather, facilitating revelatory experiencing takes finesse and artfulness, drawing people in so that they feel safe enough to venture together and respond to Spirit's nudging.

Good enough religious educators must not only help individuals seek, find, and thereby create what they need, but also assist the community as a whole to create what it needs to become more fully faithful. Morally, both needs are equally important, but pragmatically there is a priority. Facilitating the community's playing together is the point of entry, without which individuals will be unable to play. True self plays in relation to others. This is not to ignore individuals. Rather, because we are relational beings the community's playing is inextricably tied to what individuals need as well as what they can find, the matching of which depends partly on what good enough religious educators provide.

Creating new liturgies can be creative occasions for playing together, where the community approaches poetically and aesthetically some of what is needed for transformation. Unlike inherited liturgies that must be tinkered with to be made fresh, new ones provide opportunities for religious educators and participants to start with a blank "canvas" upon which to create. The community's theological, historical, and aesthetic resources can be drawn upon and/or new elements can be invented and experimented with in addressing what is called for. In the aftermath of the September 11 attacks, faith communities created liturgies and other rituals that fostered healing, peace, and multireligious understanding. Emerging churches create new liturgies that renegotiate what is traditionally given as sacrosanct. Women, people of color, and LGBTQ communities develop distinctive liturgies that speak to and draw upon their own experience, context, and LPTA to address sexism, racism, homophobia, and hate. The faithful play with new images, practices, and communal memories to shape Christian formation in particular and creative ways.

One could argue that in the community's playing, the Holy Spirit aids in creating environments in "which the frustrations of an imperfect world can be tolerated."[28] Not one among us is unfamiliar with the frustrations of the many imperfect worlds of which we are a part. The Rheinland nuns, the holy fools, the Japanese American Christians, and the incarcerated—all were or are marginalized people who knew or know intimately experiences of alienation. However, we too live in worlds where many forms of oppression abound. No matter the context, we need grounds for playing, where

28. Parker, "Holy Spirit," 190.

we experience and practice a microcosm of God's new creation, where a heightened awareness of our relatedness interrupts the fragmentation of worlds in which we participate. In shaking off at least temporarily the frustrations of our multiple, fractured worlds, we are decentered from life as usual and the ways that our worlds have deformed us. On grounds that allow playing, the faithful find support for becoming more than we thought possible or could manage alone. We are summoned by hope to greater possibilities.

Churches and other faith communities serve as unique, vital grounds for playing wherever they are. They are distinguishable from other communal grounds for playing, where individuals are drawn together to play in diverse ways. Members of a city's gay men's choir might also enjoy revelatory experiencing, as well as a community theater group. Festivals, art exhibitions, the Olympic Games, and other events provide occasions for revelatory experiencing where diverse people practice freedom and equality, inviting Spirit to be present in playing that heals and transforms. Moltmann believed that Spirit works creatively to form not only Christians but all people regardless of religious belief, gender, or age in a new kind of community.[29] While the grace of playing makes a difference no matter when, where, and by whom it is experienced, it makes a difference when people know "grace *as* grace."[30]

A COMMITMENT TO PLAYING FOR LOVE'S SAKE

This book has been a practical theological project in religious education that emphasizes pedagogies that foster revelatory experiencing. By focusing on pedagogies, the study opened to view intentional ways of accompanying learners, facilitating their playing, and participating in co-creating so as to deepen their becoming new within and with one another. The study revealed that pedagogies of playing form learners in faith in three ways—in partnering with Spirit in the creative process, in engaging the community in making tradition new and relevant, and in tending to the needs of those who suffer, including ourselves and others who wait to be "found." All of this can be understood as playing for love's sake, a notion introduced in reconstructing Moltmann's work on playing. However, this book expands Moltmann's ideas by exploring what playing and loving look like in practice.

29. Moltmann, *Experiences in Theology*, 326.

30. Gustafason, *Ethics*, 118.

Playing that forms Christians in faith involves risking oneself for the love that God first offered to us as God's own, for love that yearns for healing and transformation, and for love that binds human beings to one another. We play not for the sake of having experiences. We play for the sake of experiencing that which reveals us as able to be loved and to love more and more fully.

Playing for love's sake is a different rationale than the reasons why other communities play together. Some play for the sake of communal identity, for the sake of living well, or for the sake of entertainment. In contrast, pedagogies of playing are facilitated out of love for learners and are engaged in the hope of what the faithful can be with and for one another, to which (for Christians) the gospel points. Because learners require the support of good enough religious educators to engage this risk-taking approach to learning, educators are called upon to love through their teaching and their playing anyone and everyone in their care, including those who cannot play. This is what Jesus did. As a teacher, he played for love's sake, loving all those he taught. This is what the good enough mother does with her child and what Winnicott does when he plays with the children he sees clinically. He sits on the floor with them and participates in their playing. Playing for love's sake is what the Rheinland nuns practiced in tending to the baby Jesus and venerating Mary, and why the holy fools took such radical measures to decenter and re-center people. It is why my mother has dedicated over twenty-five years to bringing visual art to worship at her church. And it is why Masankho ventured to the detention center and risked playing with the young men.

In response to pedagogies of playing, learners are summoned to be with and for one another in ways that lean toward loving—not only loving one another but also the Spirit that makes all things new. Unlike other communal ways of playing, playing at/in God's new creation includes those on the margins, addresses historic woundedness, and pushes toward new possibilities. As in other religious traditions, Christian communities practice playing with matters of life and death, extending hospitality to present believers and continuity with those who have gone before. In particular, Christians play with the assurance of participating in what God started long ago and in what God provides in the present and has promised will be in the future.

Playing is a gracious way of becoming for both individuals as well as Christian (and perhaps other) faith communities. Playing accounts for woundedness without making it the basis of relating.[31] (This contrasts with traditional approaches in which humanity seeks redemption for woundedness.) While Winnicott saw clients in need of healing, he first approached their need by playing, literally meeting them on their level and working with their capacity to create (or not). Likewise Jesus did not condemn people he met as sinners, he related to them deeply and authentically. He met them where they were and drew them out in ways that were healing and surprising. Playing affirms the goodness of creating together, focusing on possibilities that might be embraced as they emerge in between players. Spirit summons within us hope and love of neighbor, stranger, and beloved.

Just as the capacity and the need for playing continues throughout life, so too does the need to be lovingly decentered and re-centered in the many slow processes of becoming human, particularly in maturing in faith. With the help of good enough religious educators, Christian communities have played and will continue to play a vital role in meeting this need. However, the more that Christians know the grace of playing *as* the grace of playing, that is, not simply in their experience but also through critical reflection, the more skillfully they can deepen revelatory experiencing and participate with others in many worlds in need. This is how we may lean into God's new creation.

---

31. Influenced by Cynthia Winton-Henry and Phil Porter.

BIBLIOGRAPHY

Ackerman, Diane. *Deep Play*. New York: Random, 1999.

Acklin, Marvin W. "Adult Maturational Processes and the Facilitating Environment." *Journal of Religion and Health* 25.3 (1986) 198–206.

Anderson, E. Byron. "Liturgical Catechesis: Congregational Practice as Formation." *Religious Education* 92.3 (1997) 349–62.

———. "Worship: Schooling in the Tradition of Jesus." *Theology Today* 66.1 (2009) 21–32.

Apter, Michael J. "A Structural-Phenomenology of Play." In *Adult Play: A Reversal Theory Approach*, edited by J. H. Kerr and Michael J. Apter, 13–30. Berwyn, PA: Swets & Zeitlinger, 1991.

Astley, Jeff. "On Learning Religion: Some Theological Issues in Christian Education." *Modern Churchman* 29.2 (1987) 26–34.

———. "Tradition and Experience: Conservative and Liberal Models for Christian Education." In *The Contours of Christian Education*, edited by J. Astley and D. Day, 41–53. Great Wakering, Essex: MacCrimmons, 1992.

Averbeck, Richard E. "Breath, Wind, Spirit and the Holy Spirit in the Old Testament." In *Presence, Power, and Promise: The Role of the Spirit of God in the Old Testament*, edited by David G. Firth and Paul D. Wegner, 25–37. Downers Grove, IL: IVP Academic, 2011.

Balthasar, Hans Urs von. *Creator Spirit*. Translated by Brian McNeil. Explorations in Theology 3. San Francisco: Ignatius, 1993.

Berryman, Jerome. *Godly Play: A Way of Religious Education*. San Francisco: HarperSanFrancisco, 1991.

Blanche, Erna Imperatore. "Play and Process: Adult Play Embedded in the Daily Routine." In *Conceptual, Social-Cognitive, and Contextual Issues in the Fields of Play*, edited by Jaipaul L. Roopnarine, 249–78. Westport, CT: Ablex, 2002.

Boeve, L. *God Interrupts History: Theology in a Time of Upheaval*. New York: Continuum, 2007.

Bollas, Christopher. *The Shadow of the Object: Psychoanalysis of the Unthought Known*. New York: Columbia University Press, 1987.

Borg, Marcus J. *The God We Never Knew: Beyond Dogmatic Religion to a More Authentic Contemporary Faith*. San Francisco: HarperSanFrancisco, 1997.

Bourdieu, Pierre. *Outline of a Theory of Practice*. 18th ed. Cambridge, UK; New York: Cambridge University Press, 1977.

Boys, Mary C. *Educating in Faith: Maps and Visions*. San Francisco: Harper & Row, 1989.

———. "The Grace of Teaching." *The Cresset* 59.6 (1996) 11–16.

Brelsford, Theodore. "A Mythical Realist Orientation for Religious Education: Theological and Pedagogical Implications of the Mythical Nature of Religious Story." *Religious Education* 102.3 (2007) 264–78.

———. "Religious Education Beyond the Schooling Model." *Religious Education* 100.4 (2005) 357–61.

———. "Three Modes of Teaching." Course lecture. Candler School of Theology, Atlanta, GA, July 20, 2009.

Brown, Frank Burch. *Religious Aesthetics: A Theological Study of Making and Meaning.* Princeton, NJ: Princeton University Press, 1989.

Brown, Kendall H. *Japanese-Style Gardens of the Pacific West Coast.* New York: Rizzoli, 1999.

Buber, Martin. *I and Thou.* Translated by Ronald Gregor Smith. Edinburgh: T. & T. Clark, 1937.

Bulkeley, Kelly. *The Wondering Brain: Thinking about Religion with and Beyond Cognitive Neuroscience.* New York: Routledge, 2005.

Caillois, Roger. *Les Jeux et les Hommes* [Man, Play, and Games]. Paris: Gallimard, 1958.

Caldwell, Elizabeth Francis. "Nelle Morton: A Radical Journey." In *Faith of our Foremothers: Women Changing Religious Education,* edited by Barbara Anne Keely, 43–58. Louisville, KY: Westminster John Knox, 1997.

Carruthers, Mary J. *The Craft of Thought: Meditation, Rhetoric, and the Making of Images, 400–1200.* New York: Cambridge University Press, 1998.

Caughey, John. "Mind Games: Imaginary Social Relationships in American Sport." In *Meaningful Play, Playful Meaning,* edited by Gary Alan Fine, 19–33. Champaign, IL: Human Kinetics, 1987.

Center on Juvenile and Criminal Justice. "Juvenile Detention in San Francisco: Analysis and Trends 2006." *Center on Juvenile and Criminal Justice.* May, 2007. Online: http://www.cjcj.org/uploads/cjcj/documents/Juvenile_DetentionSF.pdf.

Cheska, Alyce Taylor. "Revival, Survival, and Revisal: Ethnic Identity through 'Traditional Games." In *Meaningful Play, Playful Meaning,* edited by Gary Alan Fine, 145–53. Champaign, IL: Human Kinetics, 1987.

Chirovsky, Andriy. "Anathema 'Sit': Some Reflections on Pews in Eastern Christian Churches and their Effects on Worshippers." *Diakonia* 15.2 (1980) 167–73.

Chopp, Rebecca S. *The Praxis of Suffering: An Interpretation of Liberation and Political Theologies.* Maryknoll, NY: Orbis, 1986.

Coe, George Albert. "A Philosophy of Play." *Religious Education* 51.3 (1956) 220–22.

———. *What is Christian Education?* New York: Charles Scribner's Sons, 1929.

Cox, Harvey Gallagher. *The Feast of Fools: A Theological Essay on Festivity and Fantasy.* Cambridge: Harvard University Press, 1969.

———. *The Future of Faith.* New York: HarperOne, 2009.

Crosby, Fanny J. "Blessed Assurance," 1873. Music by Phoebe P. Knapp.

Csikszentmihalyi, Mihalyi. "The Concept of Flow." In *Play and Learning,* edited by Brian Sutton-Smith, 257–74. New York: Gardner, 1979.

———. "The Flow of Experience and its Significance for Human Psychology." In *Optimal Experience: Psychological Studies of Flow in Consciousness,* edited by Mihalyi Csikszentmihalyi and Isabella Selega Csikszentmihalyi, 15–35. Cambridge: Cambridge University Press, 1988.

———. *Flow: The Psychology of Optimal Experience.* New York: Harper & Row, 1990.

———. "Play and Intrinsic Rewards." *The Journal of Humanistic Psychology* 15.3 (1975) 41–63.

Csordas, Thomas J. *The Sacred Self: A Cultural Phenomenology of Charismatic Healing.* Paperback ed. Berkeley, CA: University of California Press, 1994.

Durka, Gloria, and Joanmarie Smith. *Aesthetic Dimensions of Religious Education.* New York: Paulist, 1979.

Dykstra, Robert C. "Unrepressing the Kingdom: Pastoral Theology and Aesthetic Imagination," *Pastoral Psychology* 61 (2012) 394–95.

Eberle, Scott. "Exploring the Uncanny Valley to Find the Edge of Play." *American Journal of Play* 2.2 (2009). Online: http://www.journalofplay.org/issues/2/2/article/exploring-uncanny-valley-find-edge-play.

Ehrmann, Jacques, Cathy Lewis, and Phil Lewis. "Homo Ludens Revisited." *Yale French Studies* 41 (1968) 31–57.

Eisner, Elliot W. *The Educational Imagination: On the Design and Evaluation of School Programs.* New York: Macmillan, 1979.

Elkin, David, "The Role of Play in Religious Education," *Religious Education* 75.30, (1980) 282–93.

Elkonin, D. B. "Theories of Play." *Journal of Russian and East European Psychology* 4.2 (2005) 3–89.

Elliott, Harrison Sacket. *Can Religious Education Be Christian?* New York: Macmillan, 1940.

Episcopal Church. *The (Online) Book of Common Prayer.* New York: Church Hymnal Corporation, n.d. Online: http://www.bcponline.org/DailyOffice/compline.html.

Erikson, Erik H. *Childhood and Society.* New York: Norton, 1964.

Evans, James H. *Playing.* Minneapolis: Fortress, 2010.

Flanagan, Kieran. "Liturgy as Play: A Hermeneutics of Ritual Re-Presentation." *Modern Theology* 4.4 (1988) 345–72.

Foster, Charles R. *Educating Clergy: Teaching Practices and the Pastoral Imagination.* San Francisco: Jossey-Bass, 2006.

———. *From Generation to Generation: The Adaptive Challenge of Mainline Protestant Education in Forming Faith.* Eugene, OR: Cascade, 2012.

Francis of Assis. *Le Speculum perfectionis.* Edited by P. Sabatier. Manchester: Manchester University Press, 1928.

Freire, Paulo. *Pedagogy of the Oppressed.* New York: Continuum, 2000.

Freud, Sigmund. *Beyond the Pleasure Principle.* Translated from 2nd German edition by C. J. M. Hubback. London; Vienna: International Psycho-analytical, 1922.

———. *The Future of an Illusion.* Translated and edited by James Strachey. New York: W. W. Norton, 1961.

Fuller, Robert C. *Wonder: From Emotion to Spirituality.* Chapel Hill, NC: University of North Carolina Press, 2006.

Gadamer, Hans-Georg. *The Relevance of the Beautiful and Other Essays.* Translated by Nicholas Walker. Cambridge: Cambridge University Press, 1986.

———. *Truth and Method.* Translated by Joel Weinsheimer and Donald G. Marshall. New York: Continuum, 2004.

García-Rivera, Alex. *The Community of the Beautiful: A Theological Aesthetics.* Collegeville, MN: Liturgical, 1999.

Gendlin, Eugene T. *Experiencing and the Creation of Meaning: A Philosophical and Psychological Approach to the Subjective.* Evanston, IL: Northwestern University Press, 1997.

Gertrude. *Gertrude of Helfta: The Herald of Divine Love.* Translated by Margaret Winkworth. New York: Paulist, 1992.

Goldberg, Peta. "Towards a Creative Arts Approach to the Teaching of Religious Education with Special Reference to the Use of Film." *British Journal of Religious Education* 26.2 (2004) 175–84.

González-Andrieu, Cecilia. *Bridge to Wonder: Art as a Gospel of Beauty.* Waco, TX: Baylor University Press, 2012.

Gorringe, Timothy. *The Education of Desire: Towards a Theology of the Senses.* The 2000 Dioes of British Columbia John Albert Hall Lectures at the Centre for Studies in Religion and Society in the University of Victoria (BC). Harrisburg, PA: Trinity, 2002.

Goto, Courtney T. "Artistic Play: Seeking the God of the Unexpected." PhD diss., Emory University, 2010.

———. "Asian American Practical Theologies." In *Opening the Field of Practical Theology: An Introduction,* edited by Kathleen A. Cahalan and Gordon S. Mikoski, 31–44. Lanham, MD: Rowman & Littlefield, 2014.

———. "Issei Garden as Performative Space." *Amerasia Journal* 38.3 (2012) 76–97.

———. "Pretending to be Japanese: Artistic Play in a Japanese-American Church and Family." *Religious Education* 103.4 (2008) 440–55.

Gräb, Wilhelm. "Church, Religion and the Struggle Against Poverty: The Issue of Practical Theology." In *Poverty, Suffering and HIV-AIDS: International Practical Theological Perspectives,* edited by Pamela D. Couture and Bonnie J. Miller-McLemore, 83–91. Cardiff: Cardiff Academic, 2003.

Griffith, Colleen. "Aesthetical Musings: Interviews with Amos Niven Wilder and James Luther Adams," *Religious Education* 76.1 (1981) 16–26.

Groos, Karl. *The Play of Animals.* Translated by Elizabeth L. Baldwin, edited by J. Mark Baldwin. New York: D. Appleton, 1898.

Guardini, Romano. *The Spirit of the Liturgy.* New York: Crossroad, 1998.

Gustafson, James M. *Protestant and Roman Catholic Ethics: Prospects for Rapprochement.* Chicago: University of Chicago Press, 1978.

Guttesen, Poul F. *Leaning into the Future: The Kingdom of God in the Theology of Jürgen Moltmann and in the Book of Revelation.* Eugene, OR: Pickwick, 2009.

Hamburger, Jeffrey F. *The Visual and the Visionary: Art and Female Spirituality in Late Medieval Germany.* New York: Zone, 1998.

Hamman, Jaco J. *A Play-full Life: Slowing Down and Seeking Peace.* Cleveland: Pilgrim, 2011.

———. "Playing." In *The Wiley-Blackwell Companion to Practical Theology,* edited by Bonnie J. Miller-McLemore, 142–50. Chichester, UK: Blackwell, 2012.

Handelman, Don. *Models and Mirrors: Towards an Anthropology of Public Events.* Oxford: Berghahn, 1998.

Harris, Maria. *Teaching and Religious Imagination: An Essay in the Theology of Teaching.* San Francisco: HarperSanFrancisco, 1991.

Harris, Maria, and Gabriel Moran. *Reshaping Religious Education: Conversations on Contemporary Practice.* Louisville, KY: Westminster John Knox, 1998.

Hart, Trevor. "Imagination for the Kingdom of God: Hope, Promise, and the Transformative Power of an Imagined Future." In *God Will be All in All: The Eschatology of Jürgen Moltmann*, edited by Richard Baukham, 49–76. Edinburgh: T. & T. Clark, 1999.

Hauerwas, Stanley, and William H. Willimon. *Lord, Teach Us: The Lord's Prayer in the Christian Life*. Nashville: Abingdon, 1996.

Heywood, David. *Divine Revelation and Human Learning: A Christian Theory of Knowledge*. Burlington, VT: Ashgate, 2004.

Hinds, Mark D. "Congregation as Educator: Problem and Possibility for the Professional Church Educator." *Religious Education* 95.1 (2000) 79–93.

Hopewell, James F. *Congregation: Stories and Structures*. Philadelphia: Fortress, 1987.

Hughes, S. *The Little Flowers of St. Francis and Other Franciscan Writings*. New York: New American Library, 1964.

Huizinga, Johan. *Homo Ludens: A Study of the Play-Element in Culture*. Boston: Beacon, 1955.

Illman, Ruth, and W. Alan Smith. *Theology of the Arts: Engaging Faith*. New York: Routledge, 2013.

Iser, Wolfgang. *The Fictive and the Imaginary: Charting Literary Anthropology*. Baltimore: J. Hopkins University Press, 1993.

Ivanov, Sergej A. *Holy Fools in Byzantium and Beyond*. Oxford: Oxford University Press, 2006.

James, William. *The Varieties of Religious Experience*. New York: Library of America: Penguin, 2010.

Javore, Barbara. "Rising from the Ashes: Aesthetic Experience and Creative Transformation," Conference paper. Annual meeting of the Religious Education Association, Atlanta, GA, November 3, 2012.

Johnston, Robert K. *The Christian at Play*. Grand Rapids: Eerdmans, 1983.

Jones, Kirk Byron. *Holy Play: The Joyful Adventure of Unleashing Your Divine Purpose*. San Francisco: Jossey-Bass, 2007.

———. *The Jazz of Preaching: How to Preach with Great Freedom and Joy*. Nashville: Abingdon, 2004.

Justin. "Justin Martyr, from *The First Apology*." In *Theological Aesthetics: A Reader*, edited by Gesa Elsbeth Thiessen, 44–45. Grand Rapids: Eerdmans, 2005.

Kaufman, Gordon D. *In Face of Mystery: A Constructive Theology*. Cambridge, MA: Harvard University Press, 1993.

Kearney, Richard. *The Wake of Imagination: Toward a Postmodern Culture*. Minneapolis: University of Minnesota Press, 1988.

Keen, Sam. *Apology for Wonder*. New York: Harper & Row, 1969.

Kelly, Patrick. "Flow, Sport, and the Spiritual Life." In *Theology, Ethics and Transcendence in Sports*, edited by Jim Parry et al. 163–77. London: Routledge, 2011.

Kerr, J. H. "A Structural-Phenomenology of Play in Context." In *Adult Play: A Reversal Theory Approach*, edited by J. H. Kerr and Michael J. Apter, 31–42. Berwyn, PA: Swets & Zeitlinger, 1991.

Knight, Jennie S. *Feminist Mysticism and Images of God: A Practical Theology*. St. Louis, MO: Chalice, 2011.

Koppel, Michael Sherwood. *Open-Hearted Ministry: Play as Key to Pastoral Leadership*. Minneapolis: Fortress, 2008.

Kraus, Richard G. *Recreation and Leisure in Modern Society*. New York: Appleton-Century-Crofts, 1971.

Kuhn, Annette. "Spaces and Frames: An Introduction." In *Little Madnesses: Winnicott, Transitional Phenomena and Cultural Experience*, edited by Annette Kuhn, 13–21. London: I.B. Tauris, 2013.

Lealman, Brenda. "Blue Wind and Broken Image." In *Religious Education and the Imagination*, edited by Molly F. Tickner and Derek H. Webster, 74–84. Hull, England: University of Hull Institute of Education, 1982.

Lealman, Brenda, and Edward Robinson, *The Image of Life*. London: Christian Education Movement, 1980.

Lee, Boyung. *Transforming Congregations through Community: Faith Formation from the Seminary to the Church*. Louisville, KY: Westminster John Knox, 2013.

Leeuw, G. van der. *Sacred and Profane Beauty: The Holy in Art*. New York: Holt, Rinehart and Winston, 1963.

Lewis, C. S. *Mere Christianity*. London: G. Bles, 1952.

Little, Charles T. "[Untitled Art Catalog Entry]." In *Krone Und Schleier: Kunst Aus Mittelalterlichen Frauenklöstern ; Ruhrlandmuseum: Die Frühen Klöster Und Stifte 500-1200; Kunst- Und Ausstellungshalle Der Bundesrepublik Deutschland: Die Zeit Der Orden 1200-1500; Eine Ausstellung Der Kunst- Und Ausstellungshalle Der Bundesrepublik Deutschland, Bonn, in Kooperation Mit Dem Ruhrlandmuseum Essen Ermöglicht Durch Die Kunststiftung NRW*, edited by Jutta Frings et al., 455. München: Hirmer, 2005.

Louw, Daniël J. "Creative Hope and Imagination in a Practical Theology of Aesthetic (Artistic) Reason." In *Creativity, Imagination and Criticism: The Expressive Dimension in Practical Theology*, edited by P. Ballard and P. Couture, 91–104. Fairwater, Cardiff: Cardiff Academic, 2001.

Luhrmann, T.M. *When God Talks Back: Understanding the American Evangelical Relationship with God*. New York: Alfred A. Knopf, 2012.

Mainemelis, C., and S. Ronson. "Ideas are Born in Fields of Play: Towards a Theory of Play and Creativity in Organizational Settings." *Research in Organizational Behavior: An Annual Series of Analytic Essays and Critical Reviews* 27 (2006): 81–131.

McDougall, Joy Ann. *Pilgrimage of Love: Moltmann on the Trinity and Christian Life*. Oxford; New York: Oxford University Press, 2005.

McFague, Sallie. *Metaphorical Theology: Models of God in Religious Language*. Philadelphia: Fortress, 1996.

———. *Models of God: Theology for an Ecological, Nuclear Age*. Philadelphia: Fortress, 1987.

———. *Super, Natural Christians: How We Should Love Nature*. Minneapolis: Fortress, 1997.

McFee, Marcia. "Primal Patterns: Ritual Dynamics, Ritual Resonance, Polyrhythmic Strategies and the Formation of Christian Disciples." PhD diss., Graduate Theological Union, 2005.

McIntyre, John. *The Shape of Pneumatology: Studies in the Doctrine of the Holy Spirit*. Edinburgh: T. & T. Clark, 1997.

McLuhan, M. Introduction to the second edition, *Understanding Media: The Extensions of Man*, New York: McGraw-Hill, 1964.

Meeks, M. Douglas. "Moltmann's Contribution to Practical Theology." In *Hope for the Church: Moltmann in Dialogue with Practical Theology*, edited by Theodore Runyon, 57–74. Nashville: Abingdon, 1979.

Méndez Montoya, Angel F. *Theology of Food: Eating and the Eucharist*. Malden, MA: Wiley-Blackwell, 2009.

Merton, Thomas. *New Seeds of Contemplation*. Norfolk, CT: New Directions, 1972.

Meyer, Pamela. *From Workplace to Playspace: Innovating, Learning and Changing Through Dynamic Engagement*. San Francisco: Jossey-Bass, 2010.

Miklowitz, Paul S. *Metaphysics to Metafictions: Hegel, Nietzsche, and the End of Philosophy*. Albany, NY: State University of New York Press, 1998.

Miller-McLemore, Bonnie J. "The Royal Road: Children, Play, and the Religious Life." *Pastoral Psychology* 58 (2009) 505–19.

Miller, David LeRoy. *Gods and Games: Toward a Theology of Play*. New York: Harper & Row, 1973.

Milner, Marion Blackett. *On Not Being Able to Paint*. New York: International Universities Press, 1957.

———. *The Suppressed Madness of Sane Men: Forty-Four Years of Exploring Psychoanalysis*. New York: Methuen, 1987.

Miyahara, John. "Dear Ben." Eulogy. Memorial Service for Ben Miyahara, Simpson United Methodist Church, Denver, CO, May 16, 2013.

Moltmann, Jürgen. *The Crucified God: The Cross of Christ as the Foundation and Criticism of Christian Theology*. Minneapolis: Fortress, 1993.

———. "The Diaconal Church in the Context of the Kingdom of God." In *Hope for the Church: Moltmann in Dialogue with Practical Theology*, edited by Theodore Runyon, 21–36. Nashville: Abingdon, 1979.

———. *Experiences in Theology: Ways and Forms of Christian Theology*. Translated by Margaret Kohl. Minneapolis: Fortress, 2000.

———. *God in Creation: A New Theology of Creation and the Spirit of God*. Minneapolis: Fortress, 1993.

———. "God's Kenosis in the Creation and Consummation of the World." In *The Work of Love: Creation as Kenosis*, edited by John Polkinghorne, 137–51. Grand Rapids: Eerdmans, 2001.

———. *History and the Triune God: Contributions to Trinitarian Theology*. New York: Crossroad, 1992.

———. "Hope and Reality: Contradiction and Correspondence." In *God Will be All in All: The Eschatology of Jürgen Moltmann*, edited by Richard Baukham, 77–85. Edinburgh: T. & T. Clark, 1999.

———. *The Source of Life: The Holy Spirit and the Theology of Life*. Minneapolis: Fortress, 1997.

———. *The Spirit of Life: A Universal Affirmation*. Minneapolis: Fortress, 1993.

———. *Theology of Hope: On the Ground and the Implications of a Christian Eschatology*. Minneapolis: Fortress, 1993.

———. *Theology of Play*. New York: Harper & Row, 1972.

———. *The Way of Jesus Christ: Christology in Messianic Dimensions*. New York: Harper Collins, 1990.

Monastery of the Infant Jesus of Prague. "History of the Infant Jesus of Prague." *Infant Jesus of Prague*. Online: http://www.pragjesu.info/en/history_infant_jesus.htm.

———. "Robes of the Infant Jesus." *Infant Jesus of Prague*. Online: http://www.pragjesu.info/en/robes.htm.

———. "Veneration of the Child Jesus." *Infant Jesus of Prague*. Online: http://www.pragjesu.info/en/child_jesus.htm.

Moore, Mary Elizabeth. *Education for Continuity and Change: A New Model for Christian Religious Education*. Nashville: Abingdon, 1983.

———. *Teaching as a Sacramental Act*. Cleveland: Pilgrim, 2004.

Morales, Rodrigo J. *The Spirit and the Restoration of Israel: New Exodus and New Creation Motifs in Galatians*. Tübingen: Mohr Siebeck, 2010.

Moran, Gabriel. *Catechesis of Revelation*. New York: Herder and Herder, 1966.

———. "Revelation as Teaching-Learning." *Religious Education* 95.3 (2000) 269–83.

———. "Revelation, Dialogue, and the Christian Community." *Theoforum* 41.1 (2010) 31–51.

———. *Theology of Revelation*. New York: Herder and Herder, 1966.

Moran, Gabriel, and Maria Harris. *Experiences in Community: Should Religious Life Survive?* New York: Herder and Herder, 1968.

Müller-Fahrenholz, Geiko. *The Kingdom and the Power: The Theology of Jürgen Moltmann*. Minneapolis: Fortress, 2001.

Museum of International Folk Art. "Miss Yamaguchi." *International Folk Art*. Online: http://www.internationalfolkart.org/collections/aboutcollectionsyamaguchi.html

Neale, Robert E. *In Praise of Play: Toward a Psychology of Religion*. New York: Harper & Row, 1969.

Neitz, Mary Jo, and James V. Spickard. "Steps Toward a Sociology of Religious Experience: The Theories of Mihaly Csikszentmihalyi and Alfred Schutz." *Sociological Analysis* 51.1 (1990) 15–33.

Neville, Robyn. "Monastic Imagination? A Pedagogical Reflection." *Practical Matters* 1 (2009). Online: http://www.practicalmattersjournal.org/issue/1/teaching-matters/monastic-imagination.

O'Brien, Michael D. *A Cry of Stone: A Novel*. San Francisco: Ignatius, 2003.

Ogden, Thomas H. "Reading Winnicott." *Psychoanalytic Quarterly* 70 (2001) 299–323.

Otto, Beatrice K. *Fools Are Everywhere: The Court Jester Around the World*. Chicago: University of Chicago Press, 2001.

Palmer, Parker. *A Hidden Wholeness: The Journey toward an Undivided Life*. San Francisco: Jossey-Bass, 2004.

Panchenko, A. M. "Laughter as Spectacle." In *Holy Foolishness in Russia: New Perspectives*, edited by Priscilla Hart Hunt and Svitlana Kobets, 41–147. Bloomington, IN: Slavica, 2011.

Parker, Stephen. "Winnicott's Object Relations Theory and the Work of the Holy Spirit." *Journal of Psychology & Theology* 36.4 (2008) 285–93.

Pattison, Stephen. *Seeing Things: Deepening Relations with Visual Artefacts*. London: SCM, 2007.

Perkins, Pheme. "Peter: How a Flawed Disciple Became Jesus' Successor on Earth." *Bible Review* 20.1 (2004) 12–23.

Phan, Peter C. "The Wisdom of Holy Fools in Postmodernity." *Theological Studies* 62.4 (2001) 730–52.

Piaget, Jean. *Play, Dreams, and Imitation in Childhood*. New York: Norton, 1951.

Plate, S. Brent. "The Skin of Religion: Aesthetic Mediations of the Sacred." *Cross Currents* 62.2 (2012) 162–80.

Proffitt, Anabel, Peter Gilmour, and Ronnie Prevost. "The Congregation as Educator." *Religious Education* 92.3 (1997) 294–415.

Pruyser, Paul W. "Lessons from Art Theory for the Psychology of Religion." *Journal for the Scientific Study of Religion* 15.1 (1976) 1–14.

———. *The Play of the Imagination: Toward a Psychoanalysis of Culture*. New York: International Universities Press, 1983.

Rich, William W. "Grace and Imagination: From Fear to Freedom." *Journal of Religion and Health* 40.1 (2001) 213–30.

Ricoeur, Paul. *Essays on Biblical Interpretation*. Edited by Lewis Seymour Mudge. Philadelphia: Fortress, 1980.

Rizzuto, Ana-Maria. *The Birth of the Living God: A Psychoanalytic Study*. Chicago: University of Chicago Press, 1979.

Robinson, Edward. "Enfleshing the Word." *Religious Education* 81.3 (1986) 356–71.

Roebben, Bert. *Seeking Sense in the City: European Perspectives on Religious Education*. 2nd ed. Berlin: Lit, 2013.

———. "Shaping a Playground for Transcendence: Postmodern Youth Ministry as a Radical Challenge." *Religious Education* 92.3 (1997) 332–47.

Rogers, Frank. *Finding God in the Graffiti: Empowering Teenagers through Stories*. Cleveland, OH: Pilgrim, 2011.

Rose, Gilbert J. *The Power of Form: A Psychoanalytic Approach to Aesthetic Form*. New York: International Universities Press, 1980.

Rudnytsky, Peter L., ed. *Transitional Objects and Potential Spaces: Literary Uses of D. W. Winnicott*. New York: Columbia University Press, 1993.

Sabbadini, Andrea. "Cameras, Mirrors, and the Bridge of Space: A Winnicottian Lens on Cinema." *Projection* 5.1 (2011) 17–30.

Saliers, Don. "Beauty and Terror." In *Minding the Spirit: The Study of Christian Spirituality*, edited by Elizabeth Dreyer and Mark S. Burrows, 303–13. Baltimore, MD: Johns Hopkins University Press, 2005.

———. "Liturgy as Holy Play." *Weavings* 9.6 (1994) 40–44.

San Francisco Juvenile Probation Department Juvenile Collaborative Reentry Team. "Program Narrative." Online: http://www.ojjdp.gov/funding/SanFrancisco_Juvenile_Collaborative_2ndChance.pdf.

Saward, John. *Perfect Fools: Folly for Christ's Sake in Catholic and Orthodox Spirituality*. Oxford: Oxford University Press, 1980.

Schiller, J. C. Friedrich von. "Letters upon the Aesthetic Education of Man." In *Literary and Philosophical Essays, French, German and Italian*. New York: P. F. Collier & Son, 1910.

Schreiter, Robert J. *Constructing Local Theologies*. Maryknoll, NY: Orbis, 1985.

Seymour, Jack, et al. "Fiction as Truth: Seeking Religious Depth in Short Stories, Fiction, and Film." *Religious Education* 103.3 (2008) 277–391.

Seymour, Jack L. *Teaching the Way of Jesus: Educating Christians for Faithful Living*. Nashville: Abingdon, 2014.

Sherley-Price, L. *St. Francis of Assisi, His Life and Writings*. London: A. R. Mowbray, 1959.

Singer, Dorothy G., and Jerome L. Singer. *The House of Make-Believe: Children's Play and the Developing Imagination*. Cambridge, MA: Harvard University Press, 1990.

Slee, Nicola. "'Heaven in Ordinarie': The Imagination, Spirituality and the Arts in Religious Education." In *Priorities in Religious Education*, edited by Brenda Watson, 38–57. London: Falmer, 1992.

Smith, Jonathan Z. *Imagining Religion: From Babylon to Jonestown*. Chicago: University of Chicago Press, 1982.

Smith, Yolanda Y. "The Table: Christian Education as Performative Art." *Religious Education* 103.3 (2008) 301–5.

Stampfl, Barry. "Hans Vaihinger's Ghostly Presence in Contemporary Literary Studies." *Criticism* 40.3 (1998) 437–54.

Steiner, George. *After Babel: Aspects of Language and Translation*. 2nd ed. Oxford: Oxford University Press, 1992.

Stjerna, Kirsi. "Spiritual Models of Medieval Mystics Today: Rethinking the Legacy of St. Birgitta of Sweden." *Studies in Spirituality* 12 (2002) 126–40.

Stone, Bryan P., and Claire E. Wolfteich. *Sabbath in the City: Sustaining Urban Pastoral Excellence*. Louisville, KY: Westminster John Knox, 2008.

Stubbs, David L. "Practices, Core Practices and the Work of the Holy Spirit." *Journal for Christian Theological Research* 9 (2004) 15–28.

Sutton-Smith, Brian. "Epilogue: Play as Performance." In *Play and Learning*, edited by Brian Sutton-Smith, 295–320. New York: Gardner, 1979.

———. "Games of Order and Disorder." Paper presented to Symposium on "Forms of Symbolic Inversion." American Anthropological Association, Toronto, December 1, 1972, 17–18.

———. "Recapitulation Redressed." In *Conceptual, Social-Cognitive, and Contextual Issues in the Fields of Play*, edited by Jaipaul L. Roopnarine, 3–21. Westport, CT: Ablex, 2002.

Thandeka. *Learning to be White: Money, Race, and God in America*. New York: Continuum, 1999.

Thomas, David Wayne. "Gödel's Theorem and Postmodern Theory." *PMLA* 110 (1995) 248–61.

Thompson, Curtis L. "Interpreting God's Translucent World: Imagination, Possibility and Eternity." In *Translucence: Religion, the Arts, and Imagination*, edited by Carol Gilbertson and Gregg Muilenburg. Minneapolis: Fortress, 2004.

Thurman, Howard. *With Head and Heart: The Autobiography of Howard Thurman*. New York: Harcourt Brace Jovanovich, 1979.

Trustram, Myna. "The Little Madnesses of Museums." In *Little Madnesses: Winnicott, Transitional Phenomena and Cultural Experience*, edited by Annette Kuhn, 187–201. London: I. B. Tauris, 2013.

Turner, Victor W. *From Ritual to Theatre: The Human Seriousness of Play*. New York: Performing Arts Journal, 1982.

Turpin, Katherine. *Branded: Adolescents Converting from Consumer Faith*. Cleveland, OH: Pilgrim, 2006.

Ulanov, Ann Belford. *Finding Space: Winnicott, God, and Psychic Reality*. Louisville, KY: Westminster John Knox, 2001.

Vaihinger, Hans. *The Philosophy of 'As If': A System of the Theoretical, Practical and Religious Fictions of Mankind*. Translated by C. K. Ogden. New York: Harcourt, 1924.

Viladesau, Richard. *Theological Aesthetics: God in Imagination, Beauty, and Art*. New York: Oxford University Press, 1999.

Volkwein, K. A. E. "Play as a Path for Liberation: A Marcusean Perspective." *Play and Culture* 4 (1991) 359–70.

Walton, Heather. "Poetics." In *The Wiley-Blackwell Companion to Practical Theology*, edited by Bonnie J. Miller-McLemore, 173–82. Malden, MA: Wiley-Blackwell, 2012.

Westerhoff, John H. "What Has Zion to Do with Bohemia." *Religious Education* 76.1 (1981) 5–15.

Winnicott, D. W. *The Child and the Outside World: Studies in Developing Relationships*. Middlesex: Penguin, 1964.

———. *The Maturational Processes and the Facilitating Environment; Studies in the Theory of Emotional Development.* New York: International Universities Press, 1965.

———. *The Piggle: An Account of the Psychoanalytic Treatment of a Little Girl.* New York: International University Press, 1977.

———. *Playing and Reality.* New York: Routledge, 2005.

———. "The Squiggle Game." In *Psycho-Analytic Explorations*, edited by Clare Winnicott et al., 299–317. Cambridge, MA: Harvard University Press, 1989.

———. *Through Paediatrics to Psycho-Analysis.* New York: Basic, 1975.

Winnicott, D. W., et al. *Home is Where We Start From: Essays by a Psychonanalist.* New York: W. W. Norton, 1986.

Winton-Henry, Cynthia, and Phil Porter. *What the Body Wants, from the Creators of Interplay.* Kelowna, BC: Northstone, 2004.

Woodward, James, and Stephen Pattison. "An Introduction to Pastoral and Practical Theology." In *The Blackwell Reader in Pastoral and Practical Theology*, edited by James Woodward and Stephen Pattison, 1–22. Malden, MA: Blackwell, 2000.

Wright, Kenneth. *Mirroring and Attunement: Self-Realization in Psychoanalysis and Art.* London: Routledge, 2009.

Zajonc, Arthur. "Cognitive-Affective Connections in Teaching and Learning: The Relationship between Love and Knowledge." *Journal of Cognitive Affective Learning* 3.1 (2006) 1–9.